Science in a Social Context

Society and Food
The Third World

Diana H. Manning
Research Fellow in Interdisciplinary Science Studies,
Middlesex Polytechnic

Butterworths
LONDON - BOSTON
Sydney - Wellington - Durban - Toronto

B—4

The Butterworth Group

United Kingdom London	Butterworth & Co (Publishers) Ltd 88 Kingsway, WC2B 6AB
Australia Sydney	Butterworths Pty Ltd 586 Pacific Highway, Chatswood, NSW 2067 Also at Melbourne, Brisbane, Adelaide and Perth
South Africa Durban	Butterworth & Co (South Africa) (Pty) Ltd 152—154 Gale Street
New Zealand Wellington	Butterworths of New Zealand Ltd 26—28 Waring Taylor Street, 1
Canada Toronto	Butterworth & Co (Canada) Ltd 2265 Midland Avenue, Scarborough, Ontario, M1P 4S1
USA Boston	Butterworth (Publishers) Inc 19 Cummings Park, Woburn, Mass. 01801

© SISCON 1977
First published 1977
ISBN 0 408 71304 6

Library of Congress Cataloging in Publication Data

Manning, Diana Helen.
  Society and food.

  Bibliography: p.
  1. Food supply. 2. Food habits. 3. Underdeveloped
areas—Food consumption. I. Title.
HD9000.6.M36 1977   338.1'9'1724   76-57237
ISBN 0-408-71304-6

Typeset by Scribe Design, Chatham, Kent
Printed in England by Chapel River Press Ltd., Andover, Hants.

Introduction

> I have yet to see any problem, however complicated, which when you look at it the right way did not become still more complicated. (Poul Anderson)

This book is mainly concerned with the world food problem. The subject is enormously complex and, since it is very much in the public eye, it attracts a confusion of glib analyses and proposed solutions. The purpose of this course is to provide a survey of some of these comments and reveal the reasons for the confusion. To do this it will be necessary to touch on some of the many related problems.

One of the reasons for the failure of the many authorities involved to reach agreement on the nature of the problem and how it should be tackled is the present Western education system which tends to train specialists. Edward Goldsmith, the editor of *The Ecologist*, in his introduction to Michael Allaby's book (1972) says of the specialist:

> He devotes his life to the study of information contained within one of the many watertight compartments into which science is at present divided. Unluckily the world (or ecosphere) is not divided up in this way. It developed as a single process, which explains why its parts are so closely interrelated. The systems he is studying are, as a result, both influencing and being influenced by changes falling within the compartments studied by other experts and of which he, unfortunately, knows nothing. He is thus in no position to understand or predict changes other than those occurring in the artificial conditions of his laboratory, from which extraneous factors have been excluded, or at best in the relatively closed systems in which such conditions are most closely approximated.

Is this view too extreme?

Certainly present analyses of the world food situation tend to center round various established disciplines, chief of which are the following:

1. *Economics*   Some authorities see the problem as resulting from the economic relationships between different countries, particularly between industrialized and developing nations.
2. *Politics*   Closely related to 1. is the view that the food problem is a result of existing political systems and can only be tackled by political reform on a world scale.
3. *Technology*   Probably the commonest and most highly publicized attitude to the world food situation is that modern technology can

solve everything and all that is necessary is more research and money to ensure that more sophisticated forms of technology are developed and these are more widely applied.

4. *Nutrition*   Many nutritional scientists see the problem simply in terms of providing sufficient protein, calories and vitamins to meet the nutritional requirements of the population.

5. *Sociology*   The social scientists tend to focus on the problem of cultural attitudes, customs, ignorance and taboos which are often responsible for inefficient use of available resources and resistance to change.

6. *Ecology*   An increasingly popular view is that the world food problem stems from the exponential growth of the human species, its indiscriminate use of finite resources and its ignorance of the complex relationships between living things.

Which of these views is the right one? Are they all wrong? Are they all partly right? To what extent are they influenced by conflicting ideologies and vested interests? These are the types of question which the reader should consider throughout this book.

Note to Readers

It is hoped that the book can be approached at various levels. Literature extracts are included in the text so those without access to the recommended reading can use it as it stands, but most of the references provided for discussion are readily available and non-technical. The most useful ones have been annotated.

There is a bewildering wealth of literature available on the subject and it has been necessary to make a rigorous selection; new developments in the field occur continuously. In view of these limitations, the user is strongly advised to keep on the lookout for additional sources of information and to keep a critical eye open for bias or inconsistency in the text.

Another book in this series is in preparation which will consider the many aspects of food in the industrialized world.

Chapter One
Humankind and the Biosphere

Relationships between living things

All living things require a source of energy to power their metabolic processes and movement, and raw materials for growth, repair and reproduction. The ultimate energy source of all life is the sun. A small proportion of incident energy from the sun (0.1%) is trapped by a group of organisms called autotrophs, which include the green plants and which contain the necessary apparatus for conversion of light energy into chemical energy which is stored in carbohydrates and other energy-rich molecules.

All organisms which cannot utilize energy direct from the sun must obtain it ultimately from the autotrophs. These are the heterotrophs and they feed on plants or other heterotrophs (which in turn feed on autotrophs). A delicate balance exists between all species based on their relationships in the 'food web', the complex matrix of predator–prey interactions, and also on factors such as climate and habitat.

On the whole, a steady state exists and the population size of a species varies little from year to year. It is determined by a balance between birth rate (natality), death rate (mortality) and migrations (dispersal). However, the equilibrium may be permanently altered by changes in environmental conditions and since the environment of any one species is largely made up of other species, any significant change in population size or density of one species will induce compensatory changes in others until a new equilibrium is reached.

Human impact on the Biosphere

Humankind has broken away from this equilibrium by radical manipulation of its environment.

Since the beginnings of agriculture some 10 000 years ago, men and women have imposed a form of unnatural selection on the species they have reared for food with the result that present domestic animals and cereal crops differ totally from their wild ancestors. To aid the cultivation of crops, people have for thousands of years cleared forests and dammed rivers often resulting in permanent alteration of the ecology and climate of the area. Human migrations have caused the spread of certain species, by accident or design, to all parts of the globe and the extinction of many others.

Agriculture involves a simplification of the local ecosystem and a constant battle must be waged against pests and weeds. Careful husbandry, rotation of crops and input of fertilizers, organic or inorganic, are required to maintain fertility of the soil. All these practices need labor, tools and a discipline unknown to hunter—gatherer communities and have profound effects on social organization. It is interesting to speculate on the impact that the agricultural revolution must have had on sex roles, land ownership, class divisions, community loyalties and the like. Much must remain speculation, but it is certain that agriculture permitted greater population density and also introduced a new type of vulnerability to famine and chronic malnutrition. Diet undoubtedly changed profoundly. The cereal crops, derived from wild grasses, became staple foods in many communities as they are high in energy from carbohydrates and easy to store, but dependence on a single crop can cause chronic deficiency diseases unless the diet is adequately supplemented with inputs of vegetables or meat. Similarly this dependence on one staple food leads to famine when the crop fails, as it inevitably will occasionally, as a result of pest attack or climatic irregularities.

Third World agriculture

Traditional techniques vary widely with local conditions. In much of Africa where population pressure is not very great, subsistence agriculture relies on shifting cultivation of small areas and the use of the hoe. In these societies, women are responsible for most domestic food production. In the more arid regions such as the Sahel, settled agriculture is not possible and most communities rely on herds of livestock, constantly on the move for fresh pasturage. This requires a totally different way of life and one which is under threat from increased population pressure and political barriers to traditional migrations.

In most Asian countries, agriculture involves ploughing and irrigation which demand heavy and disciplined labor. These requirements favor a land ownership system in which land is organized in relatively large units. Often a 'feudal' system prevails and labor is drawn from the landless and peasant-farmer classes, sometimes by hereditary obligation to the landlord.

These examples are no attempt to describe traditional agricultural techniques which is a subject far too large to cover here, but merely illustrate the impact that different types of agriculture can have on social organizations.

Modern agricultural techniques and their impact on the Third World

A wide range of agricultural innovations in the industrialized world have revolutionized production. Mechanization in farming has reduced labor requirements, but increased capital and energy (fossil fuel) costs. To get an adequate return on this outlay it is necessary to devote large areas to a single crop. Mixed farming which provides manure and crop rotation which conserves soil fertility must be abandoned and high productivity can only be maintained with liberal use of inorganic fertilizers and pesticides.

Probably the most significant advance in agriculture this century has been the genetic improvement of crops and livestock by selective breeding. Plants may be selected for resistance to pests, high yield, suitability for particular soils or climates, increased content of essential amino acids, or even for ease of mechanical harvesting. Animals are subject to similar selection for desirable characteristics, a process greatly speeded by the use of artificial insemination and 'foster mothers', into which fertilized ova from particularly favorable animals can be implanted.

Environmental as well as genetic factors are important determinants of the nutritional quality of plants and animals. As a result huge amounts of money are spent on fertilizers, pesticides, and irrigation projects for cultivation of crops and also on factory-farming techniques for livestock including the addition of antibiotics and other chemicals to animal feeds to improve growth rate, texture and color of the meat, etc.

It was the new high yielding cereal crops which heralded the so-called Green Revolution in the 1960s. The popular press were convinced that introduction of these strains would put an end to world hunger. A decade later we are told by the FAO that about 460 million people are in imminent danger of starvation, and as many as 2000 million may be underfed. What went wrong?

The ecology controversy

A big argument rages over the ecological impact of the new techniques in developing countries. It has been claimed that the new strains lead to greater uniformity of crops and reduce the genetic pool. This coupled with the trend towards monoculture (large areas producing one crop), increases susceptibility to attack by pests. Chemical pesticides are expensive, tend to wipe out beneficial organisms as well as the target species and the reproductive capacity of pests is so great that resistant mutants rapidly appear on the scene. New chemicals must therefore constantly be developed, an increasingly expensive process, and the ecological side-effects of their use are often impossible to predict.

Similarly, the high yielding strains require expensive inputs of fertilizers and irrigation water. The former can cause pollution problems when washed away into rivers and lakes and they may

3

damage soil structure. Major irrigation schemes often give rise to unforeseen ecological side effects. This extract from Allaby's book *Who Will Eat?* (1972) describes some of the unexpected effects of the Aswan High Dam.

At one time the Nile used to flood, bringing not only water, but silt to the plains. The silt was rich topsoil, washed down from the upper reaches. Previous irrigation schemes for the river, which involved controlling and channelling the flood-waters, permitted the silt to reach the agricultural land. The Dam, however, holds back all the water and, with it, the silt, which settles to the bottom. The water that is released contains no silt. Thus, while the Egyptian farmers may have water, they are denied one of the richest fertilizers there is. Not surprisingly, since no substitute has been found, the soil is deteriorating and will continue to deteriorate unless and until plant nutrients can be restored. Soil scientists have calculated that fertilizers containing the main plant nutrients — nitrogen, phosphate and potash — as well as calcium and magnesium, will be needed in the Delta within four or five years. The soil of the Delta was once considered inexhaustible. Within fifteen to twenty years there will be serious deficiencies of copper, zinc, molybdenum, boron and manganese. Where are the nutrients? They are collecting in the lake at the rate of 134 million tons a year. The Dam is silting up, as all large dams silt up.

At the same time, the flow of water into the Delta and so into the sea, has been reduced. Salinity has been a problem in the Delta for a long time, but the annual flood used to wash out the salts. Now they are accumulating. The water that does reach the sea is saltier and contains fewer nutrients. This damages the soils of the Delta, but it also affects the sea itself. We have seen already how the concentration of pollutants in a river may be increased when water is abstracted upstream. This increased concentration of pollutants — for the Nile is as much of a sewer as any other major river — also reaches the sea. The water at the eastern end of the Mediterranean now contains between 38.7 and 39.8 parts per thousand of salt, which makes it saltier than the Atlantic, which has 35 parts per thousand of salt, and it is dirtier. The Egyptian sardine fisheries have been all but wiped out. In 1965 the catch was 18,000 tons. In 1968 it was 500 tons. (*Reproduced by permission.*)

And Allaby goes on to describe other ill effects of the Aswan High Dam; increased erosion; a net loss of water caused by increased evaporation and seepage; increased incidence of bilharzia, a debilitating disease. He points out that some of these ecological side effects were in fact predicted by one of Egypt's own hydrologists who was fired for his pains; his government had no time for environmental Jeremiahs!

However, many of the arguments of the 'environmentalists' can be countered. Inorganic fertilizers need not damage the soil as this extract from Mellanby's book *Can Britain Feed Itself?* contends:

> Improved productivity does depend to a considerable extent on the proper use of chemical fertilisers. There is no evidence that these are damaging the soil, or of any tendency for our land to need larger and larger amounts in succeeding years. This is a bogy which has been used to frighten us. It is based on a misunderstanding of a common experience. If land has lain fallow for a period, it will grow good crops without any added manure or fertiliser, but the yields, which may be excellent in the first year, will fall, possibly catastrophically, in succeeding years. In such a case, in the second year a modest dose of fertiliser will maintain the yield, and larger doses will be needed in later years. But the rise in fertiliser requirements does not go on interminably. Soil analyses can show just how much should be added, and, depending on the crop, larger or smaller amounts can be used, calculated to a well-understood formula. The good farmer in Britain is not using more fertiliser on the same variety of any crop than he did many years ago.
>
> There seems little risk, then, that productivity will fall. In fact, it is likely to rise. Our improved yields of cereals are caused by the introduction of new varieties capable of using higher amounts of fertiliser. Plant breeders expect further advances in this direction. However, it is believed by many that at least half our farms — those with below average yields — could even now, by the proper use of existing technology, increase their yields substantially. A further three million tons of grain from our existing acreage is a possibility. (*Reproduced by permission.*)

To those who fear that development of new crop strain reduces the genetic pool by ousting a variety of indigenous strains, it can be argued that plant breeding and genetic engineering have the opposite effect. Not only can new strains of traditional crops be produced, but entirely new species may be developed by techniques such as cell fusion and gene transfer, or by screening and selective breeding of wild plants not currently considered as food. Since only very few of the estimated 300 000 plant species on this planet have so far been tapped for human use, the potential for discovery is enormous.

Perhaps the most revolutionary advance in genetic engineering is the possible transference of genes controlling nitrogen fixation from the micro-organisms which associate with legumes to other species. It

5

is possible in this way that partially self-fertilizing cereal crops may be developed.

The ultimate limit to plant yields per acre of land is the photosynthetic efficiency of the plant. Whilst some species (e.g. maize and sugar cane) are more efficient than most, it is unlikely that we shall be able to approach the theoretical limits in normal field conditions. However, enormous improvements in output can be achieved by maximizing leaf coverage of the area and hence, interception of sunlight. An interesting new technique which uses this principle to increase yields from fruit trees involves treatment of the young shoot with a growth retardent which inhibits branch formation and causes leaves, buds and fruit to grow on the single stem. The tree only grows to about two feet in height and produces fruit only two years after planting. Furthermore, the trees can be planted just a foot apart.

A more radical method of increasing food yields is the use of leaf protein for human and animal feed. This can be isolated from virtually any green plant by the Pirie process described below in an extract from Pyke's book *Man and Food* (1970). It is possible to visualize meadows covered with a mixture of plants, (probably many we would now consider weeds), chosen to ensure continuous green coverage throughout the year. The 'crop' could then be mown for protein extraction every few weeks.

The passage below mentions just some of the future possibilities for food production (Pyke, 1970).

> The function of meat animals — sheep, cattle, pigs and the like — can be said to be to act as instruments to concentrate protein for the human diet. In scientific terms, however, the most efficient biological system for synthesising protein is the green leaf. Nowhere is protein synthesised more quickly than in a field of grass at its period of most rapid growth in warm wet weather. In terms of the recovery of nutrients from a unit area of land, it is grossly wasteful to allow the leaves of, let us say, a wheat plant to synthesise protein and other nutrients throughout the summer and then use only a minor fraction, the seed, and discard the rest of the plant. And even when the seed has been separated by threshing, a substantial part of it too is customarily wasted — at least it is not directly eaten by human beings — in the process of milling. If the cereal grain is not used as human food at all but is fed to livestock, the wastage of the total amount produced by the soil in the first place becomes larger still. In recent years a great deal of work has been done to develop a practicable means of using leaves directly as a source of protein.
>
> The process requires the fresh leaves — many kinds may be

used — to be passed through a pulper. The leaf juice is drained off and the pulp usually extracted once or twice more with water. The combined liquid is then heated to 70–80°C, which causes the leaf protein to coagulate. It can then be separated in a filter press. The dark green, cheese-like protein usually at this stage contains mixed with it 5–10 per cent of starch. It can be used directly as food, stored in a refrigerator or dried and ground, when it can be kept indefinitely if it is put into containers which protect it from atmospheric oxygen.

So far, although the technical process for manufacturing leaf protein has been worked out in detail and the nutritional value of the product established, the further development needed to convert it into a palatable and acceptable food has not been fully achieved. Work has, however, been done on a somewhat similar process, that produces from vegetable sources a 'spun protein'.

Two methods have been developed. In the first, filaments of casein, the protein from milk, or from soya beans or ground-nuts, are prepared in an alkaline solution by forcing their dispersion through a fine spinnerette into a coagulating bath of acid and salt. The filaments are wound together into a 'tow', washed and treated with a binder of flour, gums and other ingredients. The bound 'tow' is then passed through a bath containing fat and flavouring materials and hardening agents to make it tougher or enzymes to make it tender. It is claimed that the result can be adjusted to simulate 'luncheon meat', steak or chicken at will.

In the second process, the protein suspension is extruded in the form of spaghetti and its consistency adjusted largely by means of the degree of heat to which it is exposed. Again, the final product has been made to simulate meat or various kinds of sausages.

A further attempt to short-circuit the use of animals in the production of attractive protein foods has been the elaboration of technical processes for the culture of algae for food. The principle behind this work is to obtain quick growing plant substance all of which can be used for food without the need to discard stalks, roots, husks or other structures. It is also hoped to be able to grow algae with greater economy than normal food crops. The plant usually selected is *Chlorella*, which occurs in nature as the green scum on ponds and water ways. The principle used in Japan, Israel, the United States and Great Britain where work has been done on this project, is to cultivate *Chlorella* in a trough or pipe constructed from a translucent plastic material or covered in such a way that light can gain access. Carbon dioxide is introduced and the medium in which the plant is grown adjusted to contain the mixture of minerals required for optimum growth. Again, although some progress has been made, the process has not so far been brought to the point of a fully economic yield nor has the harvested algae been successfully converted into a palatable foodstuff. One special reason for food technologists to persevere in this research is the attraction which the process would have as a means of producing food in a space vehicle. (*Reproduced by permission.*)

Dr Pyke continues with a description of yeast as a source of protein, yeast grown either on molasses or on a residue from paper-making or on petroleum — all processes as yet only at the pilot-plant stage.

The ecological side-effects of pesticides can be minimized by development of biodegradable chemicals with high specificity for the target pest. Alternatively 'biological control' methods may be used. A range of techniques has been developed which include introduction of the pest's natural predator and sterilization of large numbers of males to reduce fertility of the target species.

These are all exciting possibilities which suggest that the potential for increasing food production on this planet is enormous and that such improvements need not be ecologically damaging.

However, there are ecological constraints to agricultural innovation in the Third World. The following extract from Power and Holenstein's book *World of Hunger* (1976) discusses some of the special problems of cultivating tropical soils:

Most developing countries lie within the zone of tropical climatic conditions. Although there is no generalised tropical climate, the characteristics of fairly equable high temperatures and irregular rainfall regimes occur throughout the area. Three broad climatic regions can be distinguished. First there are the equatorial lowlands where there is no true dry season. Temperatures are consistently high and the annual rainfall average is about sixty inches, although it does not fall uniformly throughout the year. Brazil and West Africa are two regions which fall within the equatorial lowland category. The second important climatic area is that of the tropical monsoon, as typified in South Asia. In this climatic region there is a marked seasonality of rainfall. These two regions make up about 10 per cent of the earth's land surface. Finally there is the tropical savannah region, which alone covers over 10 per cent of the earth's land surface. Annual average rainfall is only twenty-four inches, concentrated in one or more parts of the year, and there is at least one dry season. Vast areas of Africa and Latin America experience savannah climate.

The impression we tend to have of the tropics is one of luxuriant vegetation and fertile, productive soils. This is not so at all. Tropical climates have several serious disadvantages for agriculture.

First, humidity is the most important factor in tropical climates, as it is humidity, not temperature, that governs rainfall and evaporation. Many parts of the tropics suffer either from continuous rainfall, which encourages dense impassable vegetation, or from heavy seasonal storms, which cause rapid water run-off and loss of the top soil layer. Rainfall intensity in Africa can be anything up to four inches an hour.

The greatest drawback is the unreliability of rainfall. Often when rainfall is seasonal it does not arrive when it is needed and as a result either planting is delayed and the growth cycle upset or young seedlings wither away for lack of moisture. The high temperatures cause rapid evaporation of water, and so storage of excess water in the wet season to be utilised in the dry season is a difficult and expensive problem.

Secondly, nearly all developing countries that are not in high mountainous areas experience continuous and intensive heat. Heat encourages the spread of disease, especially where the humidity is high. It severely reduces the pace of human and animal activity. Soil fertility is also seriously impaired; temperature affects the solubility of the soil's nutrients and the desiccation and loss of organic matter from the soil. In the Congo it has been estimated that a rise in temperature of 1 degree Fahrenheit over 97 degrees Fahrenheit causes a loss of twenty-five pounds of nitrogen per acre and unprotected soils lose one thousand pounds of nitrogen per acre — an enormous amount.

Thirdly in the tropics there is a continual struggle between conservation and degradation of soil resources. Chemical reactions such as oxidisation take place at between two to four times the speed in temperate lands. The breakdown of leaf litter and plant debris by insects, fungi, bacteria and other organisms is so rapid that one rarely finds undecomposed plant matter on the surface. Humus, the organic matter which is formed by the breakdown of the plant and animal residues of the soil, does not form easily in these conditions and only makes up some 3 to 4 per cent of the soil content. Humus is an important source of nitrogen, phosphorus and sulphur. It also binds the soil together and gives it its texture and substance. Without humus in the soil, nutrients are easily leached far below the reach of the roots of most cultivated plants.

Leaching is a very serious problem in the tropics. The heavy showers falling on poorly structured soils cause a downward movement of water in the soil. With it silica and soil nutrients are leached and aluminium and iron remain near the surface. In forested areas the nutrients are brought back to the surface again by the deep roots. Also when the leaves fall, or the tree dies, nutrients are returned to the soil. The danger to the soil comes when the forest is cleared under pressure of population. Vast areas of land can then easily be laid to a sterile waste because the natural cycle is interrupted. The soils associated with leaching are called laterite soils.

Not all soils are infertile, however. Where the texture of the soil is good, e.g. in loam soils, then they do not provide a serious limitation to agriculture, so long as they are not misused. In fact it is often irrelevant to compare the nutrient content of temperate and tropical soils, since many tropical crops either do not require some nutrients, for instance calcium, or have become adapted to the deficiencies. In other words the soil potential is not always as low as one might imagine.

Soil erosion by water is also problematic in the tropics. When the sparse vegetation cover is removed, then heavy storms can easily wash away the light friable soils, often eroding great gulleys and carrying the top soil into rivers and out to sea. Literally millions of acres of cropland in Asia, Africa, the Middle East and the Andean countries are being abandoned each year because severe soil erosion has made them unproductive.

Fourthly, most of the diseases of temperate lands are rife in the developing countries, whilst many of these countries suffer also from certain endemic and epidemic diseases which are brought about because of the extreme climate.

Malaria is the most widespread of these non-European diseases. It severely weakens those it attacks; the bouts of fever sap a man's physical strength and make him unfit for any kind of sustained effort. Hence agriculture does not receive all the care it needs and the food supply is reduced. In this way a vicious circle is formed. Weakened by insufficient nourishment, the body offers little resistance to infection. Weakened by disease, a man cannot provide the effort required to produce an adequate supply of food, and so it goes on. Before 1955, when the WHO launched a massive malarial eradication programme, it was estimated that 63 per cent of the world's population (excluding China) lived in malaria-infested regions. Now the percentage is sixteen.

Intestinal diseases, contracted by eating raw foodstuffs, drinking water or just walking in bare feet (the larvae penetrate through the skin), are common in most poor countries, as are many other debilitating diseases.

In marked contrast, the life of pioneers clearing the wastes of Siberia, Canada and New South Wales in the eighteenth and nineteenth centuries was rough but healthy. On today's frontiers of development, however, disease takes a heavy toll, both in life and energy. Progress, is therefore necessarily slow and painful. But, you may say, is not Washington for example built on what was a disease-ridden swamp and does it not suffer from a hot and humid climate as unpleasant as many developing countries? Yes, indeed. But it was made habitable by techniques and energy brought from more moderate climes. Without that outside help the environment in the developing world can be too overpowering for man to cope.

The agricultural systems in the tropics, notably shifting cultivation and wet rice farming, are well adapted to the prevailing environment. In shifting cultivation a piece of land is farmed for a year or two and then left fallow for twenty years or more. It then reverts to its original bush covering in order to restore the nutrients to the soil, ready to be used again for cultivation. However with increasing population density this system of cultivation has come under a great deal of pressure. Fallow periods are shortened and the soil is overcultivated and becomes exhausted. In parts of Africa there is still land available at the margins of cultivation which can be utilised by the expanding number of shifting cultivators. But in other parts of the tropics, the system cannot carry a heavier burden of population and there is no spare land to bring into cultivation. It is in these areas that alternative farming methods must be developed in order to restore the man/land balance and provide the necessary food.

The rice-growing regions are the major exception to this pattern. Here, because of rice's unique yielding capacity and because of the large river valleys in Asia, such as the Yangtze and the Ganges, which flood periodically, bringing down rich silt from the volcanic mountains in the interior, there are agricultural systems that support huge stable populations of great density. Rice moreover is a crop which requires very few nutrients and survives well on tropical soils without needing artificial fertilisers. Since rice areas are permanently flooded there is no soil erosion problem. There is also no need for fallow periods.

The other exception to the pattern of shifting cultivation is found in some of the mountainous areas of the developing countries: places like the White Highlands of Kenya, the Adamoua Massif of the Cameroons and the innermost basins of many South American countries. They have the advantage of a temperate climate and in many cases volcanic soils which are extremely rich in plant nutrients.

Without any interference from man, the tropical environment is not on the whole conducive to high agricultural productivity. Yet, given control of the water supply, eradication of disease and improvements of farming techniques, there is potential for much greater productivity. It is important not to overlook a number of advantages inherent in tropical climates. There can be plant growth all year round. The tropics thus have a great natural potential for multiple cropping, though this is again limited by the lack of available water throughout the year. Multiple cropping would make much more intensive use of existing cultivated areas. Already in China nearly half the cultivated land is said to be under two crops per year. In India the figure is less than 18 per cent.

In addition most tropical areas do have a sufficient annual water supply, although distributed unevenly through the year. Agriculture would be more productive if water could be stored and supply ensured in the dry seasons. At present, where irrigation is not available, only one crop can be grown during the wet season. With controlled water supply another crop, perhaps a drought-resistant one, like sorghum or millet, could be grown in the dry season.

There is much room for research into such drought-resistant crops or into shortening the growing period of existing crops. Commercial use could be made of native flora and fauna, rather than introducing non-indigenous crops or livestock which have little resistance to drought or disease. Productivity can be increased if the drawbacks of the environment are overcome — certainly not an impossible task — and the optimum use made of the main climatic advantage, the facility for year-round plant growth. (*Reproduced by permission.*)

Economic constraints to agricultural innovations in the Third World

Ecological factors are important in food production, but they are not the chief cause of world hunger. Enough grain alone is produced world-wide to provide everyone with 3 000—4 000 calories a day. On the whole it is political, economic and cultural factors which determine who eats what. These are discussed more fully in the rest of this book.

The major constraint to adoption of modern agricultural techniques in poor countries is their cost.

The following editorial comment from *New Internationalist* (February 1975) presents a simplified view of some of the economic repercussions of the Green Revolution.

'Without a reform of land ownership and tenancy, technological advance will lead to still greater social and economic chasms . . .' (Gunnar Myrdal — 'The Challenge of World Poverty')

'Where serious inequalities already exist — a technological advance leading to increased productivity is likely to be limited to those endowed with superior wealth and social status — to the exclusion of the poorer majority' (United Nations Research Institute for Social Development, 1975).

'To him who hath shall be given' (First Law of Development).

Imagine you are a farmer somewhere in the poor world. You inherited 50 acres of fertile land, and you employ labourers to help you farm it. You produce more food than you and your family need and there is plenty left over to sell for cash in the local market.

Along comes a man from the Ministry of Agriculture who tells you about the new high-yielding varieties of wheat and rice.

Being somewhat educated, you can understand what he is talking about and you can read all the brochures he leaves behind. Having 50 acres, you can afford to plant 20 acres with the new seed without risking starvation if it doesn't work. Having some cash from the sale of last year's surplus and being prosperous enough to get credit, you can afford the fertilizers, pesticides and irrigation facilities required to grow the new seeds.

You give the new technology a try and it produces a bumper harvest. So this year you have even more crops left over to sell for cash. So you plant all 50 acres with the new 'miracle seeds' and you decide to buy a tractor and a new threshing machine. You are on the way to prosperity.

Down the road from you is a small farmer who only inherited 4 acres of land. He farms it by himself and produces just enough food to feed his family — with hardly any left over to sell for cash to buy other necessities of life.

The Man from the Ministry visited him too, last year. But being uneducated he couldn't read the literature or the instructions on the back of the sample packet. And having only 4 acres he dared not risk planting even one with the new seeds because he and his family would face starvation if the experiment failed. And being poor and therefore uncreditworthy he could not afford the fertilizers and pesticides required. So he carried on farming his own land in the old way.

But by now you are producing bumper harvests from all 50 acres and so are some of your more prosperous neighbours. One

13

result is that the price of food crops falls slightly in the local markets.

For your 'less progressively-minded' neighbour, however, life is becoming difficult. He is getting a lower price in the market place for his small surplus and is finding it impossible to buy the few things he needs to supplement the family's starchy diet with a few vegetables, to save up for a son's marriage, to afford to let a child go to school.

To make matters worse, your neighbour is heavily in debt. Tempted by your success, he has borrowed money at interest rates of up to 100% to buy seeds and fertilizers in an attempt to break out of his worsening situation. Now he is desperate. And he is thinking about selling the only thing he has, his land.

It just so happens that more land is exactly what you need. You have cash to invest from the sale of your crops, and you need more land to make the most of your new machines. You decide to call and see your neighbour.

You adopt a 'take-it-or-leave-it attitude' and he doesn't have a choice. He sells the land to you cheap. Now he needs a job. And it just so happens that you are going to need more labour to help on your enlarged farm. So you generously offer him a job during the harvesting season.

Next year you bring all your increased acreage under the new seeds and the new technology. Productivity rises and is reflected by a rise in your country's gross national product per head. Development is under way. (*Reproduced by permission.*)

N.B. The BBC Horizon film *Children of Peru* (55 minutes, 1976) which will probably be available for hire from the BBC Film Library by 1977, is an excellent illustration of the barriers to agricultural development in a Peruvian village.

Points for discussion or essays

Discuss the possible impact of the beginnings of agriculture on diet, division of labor, technology and local ecology within a hypothetical Neolithic community. (Brothwell, 1969; Pirie, 1976; Pyke, 1968; Sahlvis, 1974; Tannahill, 1975)

What are the economic, political and cultural problems associated with the introduction of Green Revolution crop strains in developing countries? Would these apply to other methods of increasing agricultural output? Could unconventional food sources play a significant role in meeting the

---

food needs of the poor in the Third World? (Allaby, 1972; Borgstrom, 1973; Pirie, 1976).

Dependence on pesticides and inorganic fertilizers means dependence on scarce resources (oil and phosphates). Is this wise in poor countries? Are there alternatives? (Allaby, 1972, 1974; Pirie, 1976).

Some pesticides, now banned in the West because of their low specificity and toxic side-effects, are still used to tackle plant and human diseases in the Third World. Without pest control, 15—30 per cent of food crops is lost each year, and without insecticides such as DDT, an estimated 824 million people would be vulnerable to malaria amongst other diseases. Is the use of these chemicals justified despite their possible harmful effects in the long term? Pesticides are expensive and are supplied by Western chemical industries which can therefore continue to make a profit from potentially dangerous products after their use in the developed world has been banned. Is this justifiable? Are there alternatives? (Pirie, 1976)

Chapter Two
Production to Consumption

From field to table

Whatever one's views on the benefits or dangers of 'high' technology farming, it is important to realize that food production is only one stage in the complex chain of events involved in feeding people. After the harvest, food must be stored, transported, processed to preserve it and prepare it for human consumption, packaged, marketed and cooked. *Figure 1* summarizes the steps between field and kitchen in an industrialized society.

In the pre-industrial world most food is consumed near where it is produced so requirements for transport, packaging and marketing are minimal. However, processing, preservation and storage are essential and these are normally carried out at village or household level. Traditionally, food processing and cooking are almost entirely women's activities and involve hours of work with primitive equipment.

Preservation techniques such as drying, salting or smoking of food are found in all societies, but tend to be inefficient. In the tropics at least 30 per cent of food crops is lost to vermin, fungi and other pests after harvest because of inadequate storage and preservation techniques.

In the passage below Margaret Mead (1976) discusses the influence of sex roles on developments in food preparation and nutrition.

> Today, even in the developing world, mechanized, large-scale farming — in which men predominate — is being substituted for the traditional, smaller scale farming in which women have played an important role. There is this theory that machinery belongs to men — that men understand it and women don't.
>
> The result is that women are being withdrawn from productivity and turned into consumers only — even in areas where their labor is greatly needed.
>
> Because I wanted to put this in context I went back to the history of agricultural sciences and home economics in the land-grant colleges of the United States — for the very important reason that *we set the model for the world;* while some of the developing countries may be voting against us in the UN they're careful to have our latest x-ray machines in their hospitals.
>
> RECONSIDERING THE TRADITION
>
> The land-grant colleges pioneered in making practical education respected — but they concentrated on the education of men,

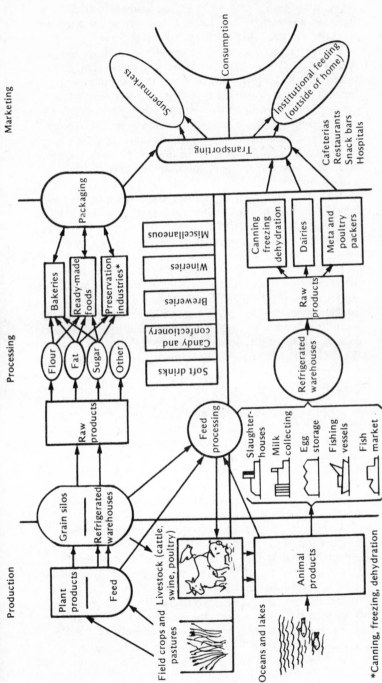

Figure 1 The food lifeline in a technically highly developed society such as ours running from production (fields and oceans), processing and marketing, finally to reach the consumers table (consumption)

*Canning, freezing, dehydration

not women. Now, a century or so ago on the American farm there was a real division of labor among men and women: *he* produced the food that *she* prepared and preserved.

In the land-grant colleges this division of labor was perpetuated. The result was that the interest was overwhelmingly in production; it stopped when food left the harvested field. Meanwhile, food distribution, storage, and nutrition, which remained in the hands of women, were ignored.

Later, when higher education for women became more common and women were brought into the land-grant colleges, the traditional division of labor continued. The girls learned nutrition, home management, and child care — in other words, home economics.

Now an interesting thing has happened. Recently, as the food industry has grown, nutrition has become of interest to *men* and so now it is considered a *science*: the men are very busy being men — as they always are when they are in a woman's field.

Home economics has been steadily downgraded since nutrition broke away. And the central discipline in home economics, which is home management, has been treated rather contemptuously. Home economics is not taught at the Ivy League women's colleges; it is not considered intellectual enough. There's a very important lesson here: whatever we want the developing countries to do we must teach at Vassar.

RECENT DEVELOPMENTS

In the home economics area, nothing has been done properly at any high level. And when the developing countries imitate us they do so by underemphasizing home management; separating it from agriculture, in spite of the fact that the whole of tropical agriculture, virtually, is based on hoe culture — traditionally practiced by women. It is the woman who knows how to gather foods, how to prepare them — who customarily handles them.

An even more recent development in American colleges parallels the one in which nutrition broke away from home economics. During the war in Vietnam, a lot of men realized they could stay out of the Army if they taught little children. Most of these men have now been forced out of the field by a system that doesn't permit men to teach little children (any more than it permits women to teach grown-ups) — but there is a residue of men who are now interested in child development, a field that has traditionally been the prerogative of home economics. *There has now been an attempt to get child*

*development courses called something else, so that men will
feel comfortable taking them.*

Happily, in a few colleges agricultural science and home
economics are being taught together in the same department.
If these few experimental programs are handled correctly,
there will be some women who will want to go into agriculture
and some men who will want to go into home economics.
Nutrition will be where it belongs — as basic science in the
whole field — but it will include studies of kwashiorkor, as well
as studies of the chemical elements in food.

HOME MANAGEMENT IN THE DEVELOPING WORLD

As long as most decisions on subsistence were made at the
village level, men and women participated together in those
decisions. There was extraordinarily little waste, there was
providence and care.

The minute decisions on food — what was to be planted,
what was its price to be, how it was stored and transported —
moved to a higher governmental level than the village, they
went into the hands of men. Because these decisions then became public life and women did not participate in public life.
But the men had no household experience.

WHAT IS TO BE DONE?

Obviously, we can't retrace our steps back to the village level.
A lot of these decisions are going to be made nationally — some
even internationally. Is Bangladesh going to grow more rice or
more sisal, for example? It's a decision not even Bangladesh can
make alone — it's made in cooperation with India, Pakistan,
the World Bank.

What we need to do is create a new discipline. We need to
take all these subjects and form them into one subject called
human ecology which would include some study of the environment, plus everything we know about scientific agriculture,
everything we know about traditional agriculture, about nutrition, and about child development.

HOW SHOULD WE DO IT?

I see two main problems in creating a new discipline of this
kind. The first is the problem of prestige and backing; highly
qualified people of both sexes must be willing to participate at
the highest levels.

Second, the key science in home economics is home management. *That* is what we need to have in the world. The great
need is *not* nutrition, in the sense of an esoteric, biochemical

19

discipline: what we urgently need is a science that teaches people how to use the foods that are there, cook them to preserve the nutrients, and feed them to the children attractively enough so that they'll eat them. Plus a lot of budgeting, storage, food preservation methods, and so on. These are the skills that are needed around the world: home management — the analog in agriculture being farm management.

I would like to suggest a solution for both problems. You get prestige in an applied field by relating yourself to something very prestigious. And home management, which is an integrating discipline, relates very naturally to general systems theory, which is also a very good cross-cultural discipline, looking at wholes. Also, it is very prestigious. So we can simply put general systems theory back of home management.

There should be some intensive research into what is presently happening. We should find those land-grant colleges that are moving toward human ecology and then see what we can do to relate this new discipline, not only to the parent sciences that are recognized — botany, plant genetics, animal genetics, and so on — but also to general systems theory and cybernetics.

The result would be a new discipline — completely evenhanded as to gender, and as cooperative as the farm was in this country a hundred years ago, when the home was a productive unit: when women preserved the food and made the clothes and men grew the major crops and both taught the children. And there was complete cooperation between them. (*Reproduced by permission.*)

Influence of the colonial era

The colonization of most of the present Third World by European powers in the 18th and 19th centuries had an enormous impact on land use and hence on social organization and food production. The agriculture of the colonies was manipulated to provide Europe with raw materials for her industries, e.g. cotton, rubber, and luxury goods, (sugar, coffee, tea and tobacco), and the switch from subsistence agriculture to wage labor and the cash economy began.

The process continues today. Most LDCs (less developed countries — yet another euphemism for the poor majority) earn their foreign exchange by the export of primary produce. Rich nations suppress competition from Third World manufactured and processed goods by a system of prohibitive tariffs.

The more processed or 'manufactured' a product, the more liable it is to import duty. For example, the rate of duty levied on three products from the Third World in Japan, UK, and the EEC are:

Japan (Cocoa) — Cocoa beans, 0 per cent; Cocoa powder, 30 per cent; and Chocolate, 35 per cent.

UK (Jute) — Raw jute, 0 per cent; Jute yarns, 15 per cent; and Jute fabrics, 20 per cent.

EEC (Oils) — Oil seeds, 0 per cent; Raw oils, 10 per cent; and Refined oils, 15 per cent.

This is discussed further in the section on world trade.

The introduction of cash crops has diverted much arable land from domestic food production and Western agricultural techniques, because of their expense, tend to be applied to these rather than to subsistence crops. The shift away from the subsistence economy and increasing mechanization in agriculture have led to a tremendous problem of rural unemployment.

Industrialization in most LDCs has copied the West and concentrated on the introduction of large-scale, capital intensive urban industries providing relatively few unskilled jobs. Rural industries are minimal because of the absence of adequate infrastructure (roads, power supply, etc.) for Western technology, so the lure of the city is irresistible and migrants flood in at a terrifying rate in search of work. The population of many Third World cities is increasing at 8—10 per cent per annum. (If present trends were to continue, Calcutta would have a population of 66 million by the year 2000). The housing problem is desperate. Many of the newcomers end up in overcrowded shanty towns lacking sanitation and water provision. Without a job the urban settler is in a desperate situation. He or she can no longer rely on home-grown food, nor on support from the extended family (Follis, 1963).

Vested interests and diet

The shift to urban living results in significant dietary changes, often for the worse. Multinational corporations exploit the naivety of poor city dwellers by misleading advertizing which frequently persuades them to spend what little money they have on soft drinks and other non-essentials. More serious is the trend away from breast-feeding induced by baby food advertising. The following extracts from *New Internationalist* (March, 1975; March, 1976) expose the dangers of this type of advertising.

The shareholders of the Nestlé company want 'a fair return on their investment'. The executives of Nestlé are paid and promoted to make profits which provide that 'fair return'. This, of course, means selling more Nestlé products.

One of these products is tinned baby milk. And as Nestlé rightly say 'the growth market' for tinned baby milk is in the developing countries where population growth is most rapid. Therefore Nestlé and other companies are expanding rapidly in the poor world and using advertising to persuade mothers to change from breast-feeding to commercial baby milk.

And so it happens that in the cause of a 'fair return', unknown numbers of babies are suffering and dying. For as the *New Internationalist* reported back in August 1973, the baby food companies know full well that tinned-milk is not as good as breast-milk and that its proper use, which needs pure water, correct quantities, and sterilized bottles, is often not practicable amongst poor communities.

The companies claim that they cannot be held responsible if people do not read or follow the instructions on their products and that it is the *abuse*, not the use of commercial milk, which 'causes problems'.

We cannot take this defence seriously. If a company enters a community for the purpose of changing the way of life and the feeding practices of that community, then it must carry a high degree of responsibility for the consequences as it would have to do in any Western country. Companies like Nestlé have taken advantage of the lack of government controls in most developing countries to evade this responsibility — with disastrous consequences.

The facts and the evidence have been placed before the baby food companies. And this has been followed up by appeals from aid agencies, churches, child-health specialists, doctors and nurses in the developing countries, and several United Nations organizations. Yet, except in rare cases like Nigeria where the government has intervened with legislation, there has been no change in policy.

All this can no longer be regarded as some accidental malfunctioning of an otherwise well-regulated system. It must now be regarded as just one more example of the 'profits before people' approach which has been built into the system itself, and which, when unrestrained, creates wealth for the already wealthy at the expense of the already poor and powerless sections of the community. When we see food companies cause suffering to children and mothers in the poor world for the sake of profit, then we are witnessing the same process which condemns miners in South Africa, tea-pickers in Sri Lanka, and plantation workers in South America, to live and work in wretched conditions for wretched pay whilst the companies they work for make 'a fair return on their investment'. And we are witnessing essentially the same system which condemned children to work down mines and committed the other excesses of Victorian England, excesses we thought had been abolished but which have in fact been simply transferred to remoter places where the crimes are less visible and the victims of less immediate concern. (*Reproduced by permission.*)

The increasing separation of production and consumption of foods in LDCs creates a need for improved preservation, transport and marketing facilities, indeed the whole 'technological infrastructure' which we in the West take so much for granted. At present the agro-allied industries, i.e. processing, preservation, packaging, etc., are minimally developed in LDCs and communications are very bad. It is the rural areas, the site of food and cash crop production, which need these innovations. The problem of rural development is discussed in the final chapter of this book.

Points for discussion or essays

In what ways did the colonial powers influence social relationships, land ownership, labor, health and nutrition in the developing world? What influence do they have now? What are the advantages and dangers of the switch from subsistence farming to cash crop production in rural societies? (Boserup, 1970; Donaldson, 1973; Sinha, 1976)

What are the causes of rapid urbanization in the Third World? What measures could be taken to reduce the rate of population migration to cities in these countries? (Power and Holenstein, 1976; Schumacher, 1973, 1975)

How might food losses to vermin after harvesting be reduced in poor communities? What technological and social changes would these measures involve? (Pirie, 1976; Pyke, 1970; Schumacher, 1973, 1975)

What are the present barriers to the development of rural processing and packaging industries for local produce in the Third World? (Berg and Muscat, 1972; Papanek, 1974; Sinha, 1976)

A biased view has been presented of the role of the multinational corporations in causing harmful dietary changes. Are there positive aspects to the introduction of modern processed foods in the Third World? Is the profit motive to blame for the present ill effects of Western advertizing or is it the naivety of the population?

Chapter Three
The Psychological and Cultural Significance of Food

People do not eat nutrients, they eat food. Food
which is not eaten has a nutritional value of zero.
(Professor J. Yudkin, Queen Elizabeth College, London)

Food conservatism and religious taboos

The consumption of food is not just a means of keeping alive. To
most people it has tremendous social and cultural importance. In the
industrialized countries we have a much more varied diet than in most
parts of the world, but, even here, people tend to be conservative
about food and many potential foods are regarded with great disgust,
e.g. dogs, rats and insects. In most communities where the diet
consists mostly of a single staple food with small amounts of others,
the staple crop is of great significance to the group and there is
strong resistance to any attempts to replace it. This resistance to
changes in diet often persists during times of food shortage. In
addition to overall food conservatism, many religious groups have
specific taboos against eating particular foods (usually animal foods)
as this extract from Magnus Pyke's book *Man and Food* (1970) shows:

> An orthodox Jew would die of hunger rather than eat pork,
> just as a devout Hindu would starve rather than eat beef. Most
> curious of all, perhaps, is the fact that a Christian, even one
> with a scientific education, who would readily accept a trans-
> fusion of human blood, or the transplant of a dead man's
> heart, would perish rather than eat the flesh of a corpse.
>   We can recognise our own strong feelings about the beliefs
> underlying the behaviour of our own society, whether they be
> the need to pay rent or alternatively the provision of housing
> as a welfare service, which can be construed as a direct contri-
> bution to nutrition, or ideas about foods which it is appropriate
> for us to eat or, on the contrary, which we consider disgusting.
> Nutritional workers and food scientists working outside their
> own countries must, therefore, be prepared to recognise, even
> if they do not share, the equally strong feelings of other
> societies. For example, a team of scientists observed that the
> diet of certain groups in the Chin States of Upper Burma was
> seriously deficient in animal protein. After considerable study a
> way was found to improve the situation by cross-breeding the

small local breed of black pigs which were raised by the farmers with an improved strain to obtain progeny giving a greater yield of meat. The entire operation, however, completely failed to benefit the nutrition of the population because of one fact which had been overlooked as irrelevant. The cross-bred pigs were spotted. And it was firmly believed — as firmly as we believe that to eat, say, mice, would be disgusting — that spotted pigs were unfit to eat. (*Reproduced by permission.*)

In times of food shortage, the range of foods which will be consumed is usually increased, but palatability is always an important factor in food acceptability and certain taboos persist to the death. Cannibalism, for instance, is very rare indeed.

Technical and physiological factors influencing food acceptability

The resistance to unfamiliar foods is not always only psychological. It is well known that in societies where milk or milk products are not consumed after weaning, there is a high incidence of 'lactose intolerance' in response to milk feeding. In this condition, the individual is unable to digest and absorb milk sugar and this results in diarrhoea. This syndrome can be very serious and is common in times of famine when well-meaning relief workers import large quantities of dried skimmed milk for the children. People, especially children, who are severely malnourished, are often unable to take solid food and must be put on a very light liquid diet containing only a few hundred calories to begin with. This is then gradually increased over a period of some weeks. The British Army actually killed many of the inmates of the concentration camps in Germany in 1945 by providing them with too much of the wrong types of food. It is interesting to note that in Belsen the starving internees were very fussy about food as this account by Mollison (1946) of a typical inmate shows:

He talked with a whining voice and complained continually, usually of his severe diarrhoea. 'Scheiszerei' was the commonest word. Second only to this complaint was unfavourable comment on the diet, the soup being blamed for the diarrhoea. Black bread was next in unpopularity. Patients who were a little less ill asked continually for white bread and complained that they were being starved. The truth was that there was enough food in terms of calories, but much of it was unpalatable. Although starving, they were extremely particular about their diet and

25

very difficult to please. Most of them did not fancy sweet things, and almost all wanted solid food rather than soup. When they wanted a drink, lemonade or something sour was most often asked for. They were all sure that soup and cold food made the diarrhoea worse. Although milk was available as an alternative to the full diet, many of the patients didn't want it, and, if given it, complained that they were not getting enough to support life.

Besides psychological and physiological rejection of certain foods, there are other reasons why unfamiliar foods may be useless to a population even when they are undernourished and prepared to try new foods. Often they are ignorant of how to prepare the new food and lack the necessary equipment, e.g. mills or cooking utensils, to get it into digestible form. This occurred during the Irish potato famine of the 1840's when the British imported Indian corn from the New World, but the people had neither the knowledge nor the equipment to prepare it properly, so even when they had overcome cultural prejudices against trying the unfamiliar food, much of it was consumed in an indigestible form which made them sick.
An important and dangerous form of food prejudice is the discrimination against women and children which is common in many societies in developing countries. Usually the men get the pick of the available food and women and children are given the left-overs.

Points for discussion or essays

In view of the food conservatism of traditional societies, why do you think Western foods are becoming popular, especially in urban communities in developing countries?

What are the economic, social and medical implications of the food taboos affecting women and children in traditional societies? (Boserup, 1970)

Chapter Four
Nutrition

Nutritional requirements

The main nutritional components of the diet, as any textbook on nutrition, human physiology or biochemistry will explain are proteins, carbohydrates, fats, vitamins and minerals.

Carbohydrates and fats are the major energy sources though both are also required as structural components of the cell, especially the cell membrane. Fats are a much more concentrated source of calories than carbohydrates, but they cannot be metabolized fully unless carbohydrates are also available. Proteins are necessary to provide raw materials for the synthesis of enzymes, structural proteins and many other cellular constituents, e.g. the nucleic acids. They can also be converted into fats, but the converse is not true in Man.

Vitamins are substances which cannot be synthesized in the body and are necessary in small amounts for the normal function of certain enzymes. Absence of a vitamin causes a specific deficiency disease and it was through these diseases and the circumstances in which they occurred that investigators were able to detect and isolate vitamins and determine their levels in various different foodstuffs. Minerals and water are also necessary and a certain amount of non-digestible bulk is required for normal intestinal action.

For healthy nutrition, food must not only contain the right proportions of these components, but must also be properly digested and absorbed which requires, besides the digestive enzymes, the bacteria which inhabit the intestine.

During World War II a great deal of interest was directed towards nutritional requirements in Britain in order to provide adequate rations for the population. Foodstuffs were analyzed and charts were prepared of the requirements of various sections of the population. These vary with age, sex and occupation. The tables prepared then are still in use with little modification, though there is now evidence that they may not be equally applicable to all cultural groups. In most developing countries a delicate balance exists between the population and its food supply and though the average adult calorie intake is greatly below recommended levels devized in the Western World, the adult population normally maintain body weight and reproduce without marked ill effects, though their capacity for work may be impaired. Children and pregnant and lactating women and the elderly may show signs of overt malnutrition but, as has been discussed in the last chapter, this is exacerbated by cultural restrictions on food intake by these groups and is not a direct indication of food availability.

This is not to suggest that there is no world food problem, but it is not always possible to extrapolate directly from our own experiences to other societies.

A great deal of emphasis has been put on the need for protein in LDCs, but as Payne's article (1974) indicates, protein deficiency is probably not the major cause of malnutrition. Estimates of protein requirements are constantly under revision and according to present recommendations by the FAO, most staple foods (though not all of the non-cereal staples) are adequate in protein providing enough is consumed to meet calorie requirements. The quality of the protein (in terms of amino acid content) can be maintained by addition of small amounts of locally available and acceptable inputs such as meat, fish or vegetables. These extras can usually provide the necessary vitamins and minerals also. On the whole, therefore, traditional, locally available foods are adequate to meet nutritional requirements providing enough, and a sufficient variety, is consumed.

Nutritional surveillance

Assessment of the extent and location of malnutrition in the world is very important if the causes are to be understood and tackled. The following extract discusses some of the problems inherent in nutritional surveillance and hence casts some doubt on present estimates (Manning, 1975).

In this paper I shall use the following definitions for the various nutritional states:

Hunger {
Starvation: Death caused by food deprivation
Malnutrition: Clinical signs of nutritional disease observable
Undernutrition: Sub-optimal nutritional status. Clinical signs of nutritional deficiencies absent, but work and health impaired
}

Assessment procedures commonly used to ascertain nutritional status of a population are the following:

1. Comparison of dietary intake with standard nutritional requirements.
2. Clinical examination of the population for deficiency diseases.
3. Anthropometric measurements, e.g. height, weight, arm or head circumference, skinfold thickness, etc. carried out in children.
4. Biochemical measurements, e.g. level and composition of blood proteins. Of these, clinical examination is the only sure way of detecting malnutrition.

But this is a tautology! Equally, by my definition of the word, undernutrition cannot be assessed clinically. It ought to be revealed by tactic number (1), but this assumes that nutritional requirements worked out for western populations are universally applicable. *Figure 2* (taken from the Club of Rome report, The *Limits to Growth* (Meadows *et al.*, 1972)), is typical of the data provided in the popular literature on this subject. According to the figure, the average African or Indian has a diet grossly deficient in calories and protein and must surely be malnourished, and yet the vast majority of adults in

Figure 2   Protein and calorie intake in a number of rich and poor countries.
(Meadows *et al.*, 1972)

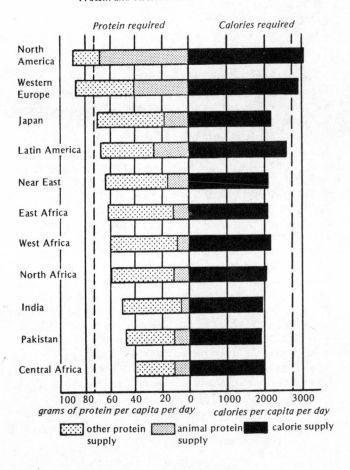

Protein and caloric intake

29

developing countries manage to maintain body weight, work and have children. It seems that nutritional requirements are not absolute. People adapt remarkably well to their customary diet and it is not always possible to apply standards worked out in western societies to other cultures.

The same is true of anthropometric measurements. These must be compared with standard tables, and these are usually worked out for western populations. Baseline anthropometric data in poor communities is very difficult to gather because of another tautological trap. We have no way of selecting a representative sample of the target population which we can be sure is not undernourished.

In practice however, these criticisms pale into academic pedantry when compared with the massive practical problems of data collection in the field: money and facilities for proper biochemical or clinical surveillance are seldom available. Anthropometric surveys are cheap and rapid and so are the most sensible and feasible screening procedures for large populations. Despite this, sampling problems invariably arise. Can you be sure you have seen a representative sample of children in the village? Could it be that the sick children are indoors? Or the strongest ones at work? Have you selected a representative sample of villages or are they the ones near the road or near the town? How accurate are your measurements? Mud, heat and humidity tend to impair equipment and small children do not always submit docilely to handling by strangers!

So there are theoretical and practical errors in present methods of nutritional surveillance. There is also one major defect inherent in all data about developing countries, and this applies as much to GNP/capita as to nutritional status. We always deal in *averages*. *Figure 2* shows the average intake of protein and calories in a number of rich or poor countries, but we know there is an enormous range within each country. There are geographical variations resulting from different dietary customs, climate, soil conditions, etc. between regions and there are variations between different socio-economic groups in the same community, and even between family members. We know that small children and pregnant and lactating women have proportionately greater nutritional needs than other groups, but they often receive the worst food. Specific taboos sometimes limit the variety of foods consumed during weaning and pregnancy, and sickness, especially the diarrhoeal diseases so common and so lethal in childhood, is often treated by drastic dietary restrictions. These factors contribute to the prevalence of protein energy malnutrition (PEM) in young children. (*Reproduced by permission.*)

Malnutrition

Vitamin deficiency diseases are rare now in industrialized countries, largely because a varied diet is available to most people and, thanks to refrigeration, canning and dehydration, perishable foods can be preserved and made available all the year round. In addition, vitamins are available synthetically and are added to many of our foods, special dietary supplements and vitamin pills are available free, in this country, to pregnant women and nutritional education is provided in schools and via the mass media. This is a recent advance. Most of the vitamins were discovered within the last fifty years and it was only during World War II that concerted efforts were made to eradicate malnutrition and that rickets was finally eliminated from most British cities.

However, in developing countries some deficiency diseases are endemic because of the tendency to rely on a very limited number of foods. Xerophthalmia, the disease which results from vitamin A deficiency is very common in parts of India and Africa where it often causes permanent blindness in children. Beri beri has appeared all over Asia since the introduction of steam-powered milling of rice. It is interesting that in times of overall food shortage vitamin deficiency diseases are uncommon. This is largely because vitamin requirements are reduced as the body adapts to reduced food intake.

The most common form of malnutrition in developing countries today is a deficiency of protein and/or calories and is most prevalent in young children. It is usually called protein—calorie malnutrition (PCM or PEM). There are two major manifestations of the disease. Marasmus, which is characterized by emaciation and is commonly attributed to total food deprivation, and kwashiorkor, a complex condition in which edema (fluid build-up in the tissues), skin lesions and various other symptoms are observed. Kwashiorkor is popularly believed to result specifically from protein deficiency. However, there is increasing evidence that the etiology of kwashiorkor is more complex.

It is probable that PEM is best prevented by a campaign which includes increasing availability of familiar foods (rather than supplying special imported protein-rich supplements) and at the same time educating the community, especially girls and mothers, in nutrition, hygiene and sanitation.

The causes of child malnutrition in the Third World are discussed in some detail in an article by Philip Payne of the London School of Hygiene and Tropical Medicine (1974). It has not been possible to reprint this article here for reasons of space, but the interested reader is strongly advized to obtain a copy before attempting to answer the discussion questions at the end of this chapter.

The relationship between malnutrition and other diseases

It is well known that malnutrition is usually accompanied by other diseases. There is a good deal of evidence from laboratory experiments on animals to suggest that susceptibility to most diseases is significantly increased by malnutrition. Furthermore, many diseases precipitate malnutrition by increasing calorie expenditure, decreasing food intake and reducing efficiency of food absorption. The many diarrhoeal diseases are particularly dangerous in this respect and are extremely common amongst children in developing countries.

Besides the direct synegism of malnutrition and infectious diseases, lack of sanitation and unhygienic preparation of food increases the likelihood of disease transmission. Ignorance, food taboos and loss of appetite often result in dietary restriction during illness so that a vicious spiral develops.

Parasite infestations are an important factor in the etiology of nutritional disease. Hookworm infestation in some parts of Africa is practically universal and this is an important cause of anemia which is very prevalent, especially amongst pregnant and lactating women. Malaria also causes anemia. Schistosomiasis (bilharzia) is a debilitating disease causing fatigue and apathy, reducing productivity and directly aggravating all the other problems. In some countries more than half the population has this disease (e.g. Ethiopia, Egypt).

Malnutrition in early childhood retards growth and mental development and these changes may be irreversible. Effectively they are irreversible because the child suffers endless bouts of diarrhoeal disease and hence misses out on schooling as this extract from a paper by Berg and Muscat (1972) points out:

> There is little doubt, however, that malnutrition alone contributes to the poor performance, to the low aspiration to higher education levels, and to the substantial student drop-out rate often found among the poorly fed portions of the population.
>
> Thus, whatever may or may not happen to his brain development at some future date, the malnourished child is permanently handicapped. He has suffered an irreversible loss of opportunity. (*Reproduced by permission.*)

Points for discussion or essays

Suggest some social reforms which might help to reduce the incidence of PEM in young children. What would be the likely problems in trying to institute these measures? (Payne, 1974)

Nutritional requirements are not absolute so it is difficult to tell who is 'undernourished' if they do not show signs of frank malnutrition. Can you think of any ways this condition could be detected? According to the FAO, as many as 2 000 million people in the world today are undernourished. What impact do you think the eradication of this type of hunger would have on rural life in the Third World?

Why is reliable nutritional surveillance necessary?

If traditional, locally produced foods can provide an adequate diet, why does hunger exist? (Moore, Lappe and Collins, 1976; Sinha, 1976)

Chapter Five
Famine

Primary and secondary causes of famine

Famines have recurred periodically in all parts of the world through-out recorded history. Mostly they have been accepted as one of the unavoidable hazards of human existence. Malthus considered them to be a necessary means of population regulation and it is only within the last hundred years that efforts have been made at famine relief and prevention.

Famine is a long-term disaster and is usually predictable well in advance. The direct cause is usually failure of the staple crop owing to climatic irregularity or disease; or the aftermath of war or other political upheaval. However, many other factors potentiate the disaster. Often there is enough food within the country, but distri-bution between socio-economic classes and different areas is inequitable. Effective relief or prevention requires good transport and communications and reliable information concerning severity and extent of the disaster. These are often lacking in developing countries.

Unless price controls are introduced, food prices rocket and people may starve from lack of money rather than lack of food. During the Bengal famine of 1943 it is estimated that some £12 million profit was made by raised food prices and 1–3 million people died of starvation. Population migrations often start as hungry people leave the country and flock to the cities in search of food. This is exacer-bated by feudal land-owning systems in which landlords have the right to evict their tenants at short notice for failure to pay rent. These migrations result in the spread of disease and in failure of the people to cultivate the next year's crop with the result that the famine is lengthened unnecessarily.

Many other factors are involved in causing famine. For instance, in times of war, the problem is aggravated by the difficulty of im-porting relief supplies. The government is unlikely to cooperate, transport and communications are likely to be seriously damaged so accurate information is impossible to obtain, the army tends to get any available food supplies, and sieges and refugee migrations add to the disaster. Modern methods of warfare, such as the use of defoli-ants and other chemical agents, directly cause famine and the most immoral aspect of their use is that they selectively attack those least involved in the war: children under five, pregnant and lactating women and the elderly.

Secondary effects and aggravating factors

Famine is inevitably accompanied by disease. Malnutrition increases susceptibility to disease and migrations, usually resulting in over-crowded and insanitary living conditions, favoring the transmission of infectious diseases. Normally deaths from epidemic diseases vastly outnumber those from starvation.

In addition, starvation has important psychological effects which result in breakdown of the social structure. In extreme cases even the family unit breaks down; children are sold or abandoned by their parents and there is a high incidence of violent crime. Normal services are neglected because starving people are unable to work.

A vicious spiralling effect tends to occur. Starvation and disease result from a combination of the disaster agent (e.g. crop failure), host factors (e.g. cultural factors, population migration, etc.) and environmental factors (e.g. sanitation, housing, climate). In times of famine these factors all tend to aggravate each other. Thus famine relief requires concentration of attention on all three.

Planning, prevention and relief

Since famines are normally predictable well in advance, it should be possible, by careful planning, to reduce the severity of the disaster. Strong organization is required, stockpiling of food should be carried out if possible, price controls on food are essential and a rationing system should be prepared.

Relief work requires information on the extent and severity of the disaster which is not easily obtained. It is important that an assessment team should examine representative communities in the disaster area and carry out surveys of nutritional status. These are best carried out on the children using anthropometric measures, e.g. height, weight, and arm circumference. It is not always possible to detect extreme malnutrition in a community since the most badly ill are likely to be indoors and out of sight. The following passage from Pyke's *Man and Food* (1970) concerning the Dutch famine of World War II illustrates this:

> The ecstatic people in the streets of liberated western Holland looked thin but flushed with emotion. 'We had expected,' wrote the reporter on the London *Times* 'to find the most horrible conditions . . . . but we did not need the special teams which stood by ready for action . . . . There were some cases of advanced malnutrition, but no cases of actual starvation'. The 18 000 dead from hunger in the four big towns and the rows of pitiful patients, some of the many hundreds under

treatment for starvation and hunger oedema in the wards of the hospitals, were not there cheering in the streets.

Once accurate information of the requirements of the population is acquired, appropriate relief supplies may be sent in. It is usually best to provide familiar food to most people rather than expensive high protein supplements which may not be acceptable. At the same time, adequate shelter, sanitation and water must be provided and immunization campaigns may be necessary.

It is important that long-term rehabilitation is not forgotten and this may require training local people in agricultural techniques and providing suitable equipment.

Points for discussion or essays

Discuss the Irish potato famine as a case study of a famine, its causes, relief efforts and long-term consequences. What lessons relevant to modern famines can be drawn from this? (Woodham Smith, 1964)

How would you set about organizing famine relief in a rural area of a developing country if you were in charge of the budget and activities of an international relief organization? (Manning, 1976)

If famine is seldom a result of overall food shortage and is predictable well in advance, how might it be prevented? (Manning, 1976; Pyke, 1970; Sinha, 1976)

Chapter Six
Economic Relations Between Rich and Poor Countries

It should be apparent from the rest of this book that world hunger is primarily a result of the desperately uneven distribution of resources between rich and poor countries and between rich and poor in the same country. There are still no signs of a significant co-operative effort on a world scale to reduce these inequalities. Donaldson in his book *Worlds Apart: The Economic Gulf Between Nations* (1973) discusses the reasons for this maldistribution of wealth and argues that, unless the economic relationships between nations are drastically changed, the gulf must inevitably increase. Tables taken from the book show the scale of some of these inequalities (Table 1).

World trade

Figure 3 and the following extract from Borgstrom's book (1973) indicate the power of the rich nations in the world food trade.

> Excess purchasing power among the affluent is largely dictating the flow of food items in the world market. Hams from Canada, Poland, Denmark and the Netherlands weigh the shelves of United States food markets. No less than 500 kinds of cheese are also found there. Beer is moving back and forth across the world despite variations in types being only minor; no fewer than forty foreign beers enter the United States market. A lively flow of delicatessen items to, from and between nations goes on, despite hunger and poverty being the lot of the majority or sizable minorities in most countries. Another glaring example of opulent preemption in food is shrimp, collected for the United States market from seventy countries, many of which are seriously malnourished. In this luxury category we also find strawberries flown from California to Scandinavia, king crab from Alaska to New York and France, Canadian lobster to West European countries. These are only a few random samples.
> During a couple of years in the 1960's Holland was the leading importer of dried skim milk and alone purchased more than the hungry world got through UNICEF and other aid programs. The dried skim milk (nonfat milk solids) was used to produce veal, which Holland in turn exported to Italy. This trade still goes on but on a smaller scale. The top-ranking

Table 1 Tables from Donaldson (1973)

1 Gross national product per capita 1968 (US dollars)

USA	3980	Turkey	310
Sweden	2620	Iran	310
Switzerland	2490	Jordan	260
Canada	2460	Brazil	250
Denmark	2070	Paraguay	230
Australia	2070	Rhodesia	220
New Zealand	2000	Zambia	220
UK	1790	Ceylon	180
Israel	1360	Korea (South)	180
Japan	1190	Ghana	170
Venezuela	950	Bolivia	150
Argentina	820	Kenya	130
Mexico	530	Uganda	110
Chile	480	India	100
Jamaica	460	Pakistan	100
Peru	380	Tanzania	80
Malaysia	330	Ethiopia	70

Source: World Bank Atlas, 1970

2 Infant mortality rate per 1000 births

Japan	15	Peru	62	Indonesia	87
UK	19	Mexico	66	Chile	92
USA	21	Burma	66	UAR	119
Syria	25	Philippines	72	India	139
USSR	26	Colombia	78	Pakistan	142
Thailand	28	Algeria	86	Tanzania	160.5

Source: UN Demographic Yearbook, 1969.

3 Daily calorie and protein consumption

Country	Daily calorie intake per capita	Daily total protein level of intake per capita (grams per day)
USA	3200	95.6
UK	3150	87.5
Chile	2830	81.8
UAR	2810	80.8
Brazil	2690	66.3
Syria	2600	77.9
Mexico	2550	65.7
Japan	2460	74.7
S. Korea	2390	70.5
Peru	2340	54.1
Ivory Coast	2290	52.3
Colombia	2200	48.9
Nigeria	2180	59.3
Ghana	2160	48.6
Kenya	2120	64.4
Tanzania	2080	58.1
Philippines	2000	50.5
Iran	1890	49.8
Algeria	1870	51.7
India	1810	45.4

Source: FAO, The State of Food and Agriculture, 1969—70

Figure 3 Meat (fresh, chilled or frozen, but not including poultry and horse-meat) — the global trade. Note that only 5.5 per cent of the meat moves to recipients other than North America, Europe and Japan.

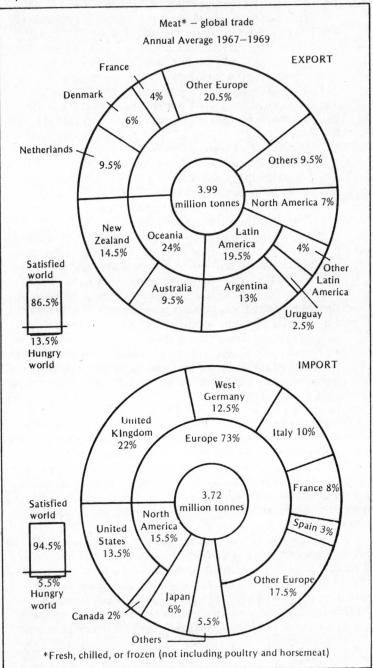

agriculture of Denmark received in the latter half of the 1960's an amount of protein exceeding 250 lbs per person annually, six times what the average Dane got through his high-quality diet during the same period. Peanuts from tropical Africa and feed grain and soybeans from the United States thus make significant contributions to the food production of Denmark. The same quaint conditions prevail in several Western nations, even though the proportions may not be as exaggerated.

Thus a picture emerges of a world where, despite all the rhetoric about battling world hunger, the lion's share of the food and feed moving in world trade is streaming into the well-fed Western world:

> One-half of all beans and peas
> More than one-half of the wheat
> Three-fourths of the corn
> Three-fifths of the soybeans
> Nine-tenths of the peanuts (groundnuts)
> Three-fourths of the oilseed cake

Nevertheless we Westerners maintain the illusion that Europe is self-sustaining. Despite the hard-pressed food situation for two-thirds of mankind, Western Europe is the receiver of more than half of the United States wheat deliveries to the world household and gets considerably more than India. England alone gets twelve times as much grain per person as India. On top of this, a large part of this import is used in the United Kingdom for the number one position as beef importer in the world and is the biggest importer of fish and shellfish, far out-distancing all other nations (*sic*). One-tenth of the protein in the ocean catch is absorbed by the United States. (*Reproduced by permission.*)

The dominance of the industrialized world in determining terms of trade has been referred to earlier (Chapter 2). Developing countries are still dependent on the export of primary commodities: minerals, fossil fuels and agricultural products. The latter have been particularly vulnerable to price fluctuations due to changes in supply (which is subject to weather conditions) and demand (which may be drastically reduced by development of synthetic alternatives, e.g. to sisal or rubber).

The formation of producer cartels has had an enormous impact on relations between rich and poor worlds. OPEC (the Organisation of Petroleum Exporting Countries) is, of course, the most spectacular example of 'producer power'. LDCs without indigenous oil supplies have been disastrously affected by the rise in oil prices and the possible formation of a similar cartel of phosphate producers would also be damaging to LDCs by increasing fertilizer prices. However, these moves have raised the morale and militancy of the Third World and other producer cartels are emerging (Sinha, 1976):

> Another important factor in the rise in commodity prices was the growing confidence in developing countries (in the wake of the success of the OPEC countries in raising the price of petroleum) and their efforts to maximise their own market power by forming cartels. This was followed by the seven leading bauxite exporters forming the International Bauxite Association (IBA). Four leading copper producers formed the International Council of Copper Exporting Countries (CIPEC). After expiry of the International Coffee Agreement the major coffee producers, through a series of interlocking marketing companies and stockpile financing arrangements, sought to obtain greater control over world coffee prices. Similarly, the tin producers attempted to increase the guaranteed floor price through the International Tin Agreement. Five leading banana producers started levying sizeable duties on banana exports. The four major tea producers began to coordinate their marketing arrangements and to establish a floor price in a more meaningful way.

Confrontation between the rich and poor nations over terms of trade now seems inevitable as the LDCs become more vocal and united in their call for a New Economic Order. The Lomé Convention was a move in this direction (Sinha, 1976):

> The Convention (signed on 28 February 1975) between the EEC and forty-six developing countries in Africa, the Caribbean and the Pacific (ACP) is symbolic of the recent changes in attitude of the developed countries, particularly the Europeans, towards the commodity problems of the developing countries. The convention aims at an integrated scheme incorporating trade, aid, the stabilization of export earnings, cooperation in agriculture and industrial development, the transfer of technology, improving economic and social infrastructure, capital movements, etc.

UNCTAD (the UN Conference on Trade and Development) is discussing broader changes along these lines, but is likely to meet with opposition from the dominant powers.

World trade in grain is of crucial significance to the developing countries and the erratic price fluctuations of recent years have been particularly damaging to them. It is effectively controlled by the rich world, especially the USA, the major grain exporter. As long as free market forces reign supreme, grain will go where the money is, not where the need is. At present, a high proportion of the world's grain is fed to livestock. Howard Wagstaff in a recent Fabian Society pamphlet *World Food: A Political Task* (1976) comments cynically:

> If there are shortages our broiler chicken industry can easily outbid the Calcutta slum dweller.

He criticizes the naive belief of many Western liberals that, in view of the 1972/3 world grain shortage, wealthy importers like the UK should aim at greater agricultural self sufficiency. On the contrary, he claims that there was no absolute shortage and that the importing nations should group together to exert pressure on the USA for a change in the organization of the world grain market. He recommends the setting up of an international grain authority to control the market, stockpile supplies and ensure price stability.

Development assistance and food aid

Development aid from the industrialized world falls far short of the UN target of 1 per cent of GNP, and the strings attached to such aid are notorious. Much is private investment from which profits are repatriated, some take the form of loans and most aid requires the recipient country to purchase equipment from the donor, thus providing a market for the products of the latter. According to Brian Easlea (1973):

> . . . Whereas the net flow of income during the years 1960—65 from the United States to the minor capitalist countries was positive, from the United States to the underdeveloped countries the net flow was negative. In fact, as Magdoff has pointed out, nearly three times as much money was transferred from the underdeveloped countries to the United States as in the reverse direction.

Food aid also has strings attached (Sinha, 1976):

> In its early stages US food aid was given in the form of concessional sales payable in local currencies. This provision went a long way towards relieving the foreign exchange difficulties of food deficit countries. However, the terms of these sales stipulated that at least 50% of food aid commodities had to be shipped in US vessels. Often US freight rates were higher than the ruling international freight rates. The US embassy and other expenses incurred in the recipient country were also met out of the income received from these sales. Therefore, the

actual saving of foreign exchange was much less than the face value of the food.

Food aid has always been used as a means of getting rid of embarrassing surpluses without releasing them on the world market. This has led to inclusion of some bizarre items, e.g. cotton and tobacco, under the label of food aid. These, needless to say, have not fed the hungry and have sometimes damaged local industries. There is always a danger that food aid may lower food prices and depress local production unless strict price controls are maintained. It is difficult to ensure that such food will get through to the needy and dependence on it can be dangerous, especially as the USA has openly admitted that it will use food as a political weapon.

No-one would claim that food aid is a solution to world hunger, but administrative and cultural factors limit its usefulness even as a short term expedient. Some of these problems are discussed in an interesting article by Muller (1974). Space limitations prevent inclusion of a reprint here, but the paper, published in *New Scientist*, is strongly recommended.

Points for discussion or essays

To what extent is hunger in the poor world a consequence of the extravagance of the rich, industrialized nations? Would the Third World benefit if major food importers like Britain were to become self-sufficient in food? (*The Ecologist*, 1972; Ritson, 1975; Wagstaff, 1976)

How significant to world hunger is the inequitable distribution of natural resources between countries? Does the world grain trade influence what poor people eat?

Discuss the benefits and problems of food aid. What are the political and administrative impediments to its efficiency? Does it have a role to play in tackling malnutrition? (Donaldson, 1973; Power and Holenstein, 1976)

The common factor in these discussion questions is the gulf between the decision makers and the majority in LDCs. The former tend to be rich, educated, Westernized, urban and male and hence are a highly unrepresentative elite. However well-meaning they may be, they are separated from the masses by enormous differences in wealth, culture, outlook, ethnic loyalties, language and also poor technological communications. In addition they tend to have vested

---

interests in the status quo. Changes in world trade seem inevitable as Third World countries become more militant and organized, but how will a more favorable trading position affect the lives of the poorest 40% of the population?

Chapter Seven
Strategies for Rural Development

Whatever the future of world food trade and aid, most authorities agree that ideally developing countries should provide a basic, adequate diet for their people from their own resources.

To ensure that people are fed they must either have enough land to grow their own, or enough money to buy it. They also need knowledge, equipment and motivation to grow, store and prepare food as efficiently and hygienically as possible and eat sufficient quantity and variety of available foods to meet nutritional requirements.

It sounds simple, but actually involves nothing short of a revolution in rural life.

Land

As Frances Moore Lappe and Joe Collins (1976) point out every country has sufficient agricultural land to provide an adequate diet for its population. But in most LDCs land ownership is far from equitable. Many authorities see land reform as a basic prerequisite to rural development, but there are many problems involved. Land redistribution is difficult to implement and may not redress the balance of power between the privileged and the poor. Sinha in his book *Food and Poverty* (1976, pp. 48–65) discusses the various types of land reform including nationalization and collectivization.

All types give rise to administrative problems, particularly in the provision of credit and marketing facilities which must accompany land redistribution. Administrators tend to be drawn from the educated, urban minority and are therefore ill-equipped to communicate with and understand the problems of illiterate peasant farmers. Poor communications impede the enforcement of any new legislation in remote areas and hamper the evaluation of its effects. Sinha reckons these problems can only be overcome by greater peasant participation in the implementation of any reform.

Employment: the 'Hard' vs 'Soft' technology controversy

With or without land reform there is a tremendous need for job creation in LDCs. Conventional development strategies have concentrated on rapid industrialization along Western lines. The tendency

45

for land to be concentrated in fewer hands permits greater mechanization and hence higher productivity and the surplus labor displaced from the land, so the argument goes, should then be absorbed in manufacturing industry in the urban sector. The massive unemployment problem and the explosive growth of impoverished squatter communities in the cities of most LDCs suggest that this tactic is not working.

The following extracts from Schumacher's influential book *Small is Beautiful* (1973, 1975) argue the case for a new approach to industrialization in the Third World:

DEFINITION OF INTERMEDIATE TECHNOLOGY

If we define the level of technology in terms of 'equipment cost per workplace', we can call the indigenous technology of a typical developing country — symbolically speaking — a £1-technology, while that of the developed countries could be called a £1,000-technology. The gap between these two technologies is so enormous that a transition from the one to the other is simply impossible. In fact, the current attempt of the developing countries to infiltrate the £1,000-technology into their economies inevitably kills off the £1-technology at an alarming rate, destroying traditional workplaces much faster than modern workplaces can be created, and thus leaves the poor in a more desperate and helpless position than ever before. If effective help is to be brought to those who need it most, a technology is required which would range in some intermediate position between the £1-technology and the £1,000-technology. Let us call it — again symbolically speaking — a £100-technology.

Such an intermediate technology would be immensely more productive than the indigenous technology (which is often in a condition of decay), but it would also be immensely cheaper than the sophisticated, highly capital-intensive technology of modern industry. At such a level of capitalisation, very large numbers of workplaces could be created within a fairly short time; and the creation of such workplaces would be 'within reach' for the more enterprising minority within the district, not only in financial terms but also in terms of their education, aptitude, organising skill, and so forth.

This last point may perhaps be elucidated as follows:

The average annual income per worker and the average capital per workplace in the developed countries appear at present to stand in a relationship of roughly 1:1. This implies, in general terms, that it takes one man-year to create one workplace, or that a man would have to save one month's earnings a year for twelve years to be able to own a workplace. If the relationship were 1:10, it would require ten man-years to create one work-place, and a man would have to save a month's earnings a year for 120 years before he could make himself owner of a work-place. This, of course, is an impossibility, and it follows that the £1,000-technology transplanted into a district which is stuck on the level of a £1-technology simply cannot spread by any process of normal growth. It cannot have a positive 'demonstration effect'; on the contrary, as can be observed all over the world, its 'demonstration effect' is wholly negative. The people, to whom the £1,000-technology is inaccessible. simply 'give up' and often cease doing even those things which they had done previously.

The intermediate technology would also fit much more smoothly into the relatively unsophisticated environment in which it is to be utilised. The equipment would be fairly simple and therefore understandable, suitable for maintenance and repair on the spot. Simple equipment is normally far less dependent on raw materials of great purity or exact specifications and much more adaptable to market fluctuations than highly sophisticated equipment. Men are more easily trained; super-vision, control, and organisation are simpler; and there is far less vulnerability to unforeseen difficulties.

THE NATURE OF THE TASK

The task, then, is to bring into existence millions of new work-places in the rural areas and small towns. That modern industry, as it has arisen in the developed countries, cannot possibly fulfil this task should be perfectly obvious. It has arisen in societies which are rich in capital and short of labour and therefore can-not possibly be appropriate for societies short of capital and rich in labour. Puerto Rico furnishes a good illustration of the point. To quote from a recent study:

> Development of modern factory-style manufacturing makes only a limited contribution to employment. The Puerto Rican development programme has been unusually vigorous and successful; but from 1952—62 the average increase of employment in EDA-sponsored plants was about 5000 a year. With present labour force participation rates, and in the absence of net emigration to the main-land, annual additions to the Puerto Rican labour force would be of the order of 40 000 . . .
> Within manufacturing, there should be imaginative exploration of small-scale, more decentralised, more labour-using forms of organisation such as have persisted

47

in the Japanese economy to the present day and have contributed materially to its vigorous growth.

Equally powerful illustrations could be drawn from many other countries, notably India and Turkey, where highly ambitious five-year plans regularly show a greater volume of unemployment at the end of the five-year period than at the beginning, even assuming that the plan is fully implemented.

The real task may be formulated in four propositions:

First, that workplaces have to be created in the areas where the people are living now, and not primarily in metropolitan areas into which they tend to migrate.

Second, that these workplaces must be, on average, cheap enough so that they can be created in large numbers without this calling for an unattainable level of capital formation and imports.

Third, that the production methods employed must be relatively simple, so that the demands for high skills are minimised, not only in the production process itself but also in matters of organisation, raw material supply, financing, marketing, and so forth.

Fourth, that production should be mainly from local materials and mainly for local use.

These four requirements can be met only if there is a 'regional' approach to development and, second, if there is a conscious effort to develop and apply what might be called an 'intermediate technology'. (*Reproduced by permission.*)

The call for 'appropriate technology' (AT) has been taken up by the environmentalist lobby who are concerned about the ecological impact of Western technology in the Third World. The *Ballad of Ecological Awareness* (Boulding, 1973) is a humorous illustration of this attitude. The ecological implications of agricultural change in the tropics are discussed in Chapter 1.

The political implications of AT are enormous. If it is introduced as a 'technological fix' it is likely to be taken over by the already privileged. However, it can be used as a tool to assist radical change in rural social organization, permitting self sufficiency in basic necessities at a local level and communal control over the means of production. Such has been its role in the Chinese communes, the ujamaa villages of Tanzania, and the Ghandian movement in India.

Self help movements, however, can only gain momentum if the initiative comes from the local populace itself. At present most of the research and enthusiasm for AT comes from the West (Manning, 1976):

The problem is how to get the great mass of the rural population interested in taking initiative to develop or adopt new technologies which optimise use of local resources to meet local needs. Education of a minority in design skills is simply not enough. One clue to the problem of rural inertia is the role of women in traditional society. Mostly they are excluded from public life, community affairs, formal education, etc., but have control over most subsistence activities such as food processing and preparation, child care, water collection, provision for health and hygiene, and often subsistence agriculture. Women thus constitute the 'hard core' of traditional society, with responsibility for the most basic processes of survival and yet they are the most conservative and inaccessible half of the population. Present research by the Intermediate Technology Development Group and other organisations into AT for rural development has produced some inspired inventions for improving clean water provision, better storage methods for foodstuffs (and, since more than 30 per cent of food crops in LDCs is lost to pests after harvesting, this is extremely important) and methods of food processing, e.g. threshing and milling, which could eliminate hours of drudgery. However, these innovations apply mainly to women's work and will not be adopted unless women are educated to use them and appreciate their advantages. Ideally, local women should participate in the design of such equipment if rural development is to gather its own momentum, but the barriers to such a move are enormous.

In general, AT will only catch on in rural societies if the local population are prepared in terms of attitudes and skills to use, and preferably contribute to the design of, new technologies most appropriate to their particular situation. (*Reproduced by permission.*)

There can be no doubt that any attempts to 'politicize' the rural majority will meet with massive opposition from the ruling elites in most LDCs, who have vested interests in the present system. Furthermore, Western nations (and the Soviet Bloc) have a powerful interest in ensuring a continuing cheap supply of raw materials from the Third World and multinational companies use LDCs as a source of cheap labor and a market for their products.

Besides overt self-interest, there are ideological objections to the formation of small-scale, self help, rural collectives. In a paper passionately upholding American values, Henry Luce (1966) makes the following comments about the world food situation:

You recall that only a few years ago there appeared a number of books with titles like 'Our Plundered Planet'. They greatly impressed many intellectuals and other refined gentry. These books argued that even if the race of man were not destroyed by atomic bombs, it would soon fade away from lack of agricultural resources. Such a thesis fitted old thought patterns, however dressed up with scientific data. With all respect for my betters, I thought it was nonsense. It did not take account of the blazing new fact — that we have opened the door into a universe of boundless energy. Energy which can be used for boundless better or boundless worse, but inexhaustible energy.

Our problems are problems of abundance. I stress this new fact of life but I couple it with an ancient truth. Contrary to so much modern thinking, it is not material conditions which are most important to human welfare; what is most important are the political institutions and the philosophy of faith which inform them. What men and nations make of themselves depends on what they deeply think they were born to be.

COMMUNISM CANNOT PRODUCE FOOD

This leads me to third generalization — one that is inescapable today in any symposium concerned with food. The generalization is that Communism is utterly incompatible with the production of food. Communism may or may not have bloody-red hands, but it certainly does not have green thumbs. Perhaps Communism is incompatible with the efficient production of anything, but it certainly cannot grow abundance of food.

The food failure in Russia must be rated as one of the most extraordinary events in all history. And I should like to suggest that it is something unique, that rarest of things, a clear lesson in history. (I leave aside the appalling catastrophe of China as being too tragic to be discussed in any dispassionate manner.)

INCENTIVE IS ESSENTIAL

. . . the way to increase agricultural production in an Indian village is to provide it with a supermarket or at least with a Sears, Roebuck catalogue. Men and women need to be shown what they can get, besides coffee, by more work more intelligently done. (*Reproduced by permission.*)

Support for the 'Hard' technology approach to development comes also from those who see world hunger as a problem of inadequate food production. The assumption is that if sophisticated technology is applied to maximizing food production, and maintaining a high rate of economic growth, that eventually the benefits will filter down to the poor majority without a radical redistribution of wealth. An excellent illustration of this view is to be found in the film *Food or Famine*, available from the Shell film library (1970).

Education

Changes in rural agriculture, food preparation, food habits, hygiene, rural industries and so on require appropriate education. Western-type schooling is expensive, specialized and often innaccessible to the majority. Children, particularly girls, in traditional rural societies are required to work at home, so the drop-out rate is high. The privileged few who get through to secondary and tertiary education tend to have western aspirations and seek prestigious employment in the cities. Formal education is not an appropriate vehicle for instruction in agriculture/nutrition/health/family planning, etc. because it is academic, elitist, expensive and reaches only a tiny proportion of the population.

The alternative, nonformal education, includes a ragged mixture of extension services, vocational training, adult education courses, co-operative self-help schemes and integrated development projects. Between them they aim to provide basic education in literacy and numeracy, family improvement (health, nutrition etc.), community improvement (government, administration, etc.), and occupational skills.

The diverse schemes now underway show signs of success, but often the improvements are temporary. After the first enthusiasm, recruitment wanes, there are staffing problems and the inertia of traditional society takes over once more. The following are some of the reasons why nonformal education programs seldom maintain their initial impetus.

1. *Objectives:* These are usually too ambitious. For rural inertia to change is a very great step so aims must be kept as simple and realistic as possible.
2. *Technology:* Certain types of modern technology e.g. radio, films, etc. can be very useful as educational aids, but the technology used must be appropriate to the country and the content of the program. Experience has shown that radio is an exceptionally good medium for instruction in nutrition, health and agriculture, but that literacy projects require posters, texts and teacher/learner contact. Extravagant media, such as video and TV, seldom justify their expense.
3. *Recruitment:* Projects which require residential training and fees only reach the highly motivated and those free to leave their home responsibilities for weeks at a time. Agricultural extension services also tend to reach the progressive minority. Most projects are aimed primarily at men and the few that are for women are normally limited to Home Economics instruction, despite the widespread involvement of women in agriculture, home industry and trade.

Adequate evaluation of response to the projects is seldom

carried out and there are not usually any follow-up or refresher courses to consolidate the new information.

4. *Staffing:* The administrative hierarchy involved in these projects is complex and bureaucratic and, as usual, the people who actually do the field work are the least qualified and least well paid. Conditions of service are often bad and the best of the field workers are promoted to administrative posts. Communication between the decision makers in their urban offices and the field workers is usually bad and adequate evaluation of the projects is thus impossible.

5. *Content:* This must be pretested for suitability in the target population. Where possible it should be put over in the local vernacular and should not presuppose literacy. Above all, it must be kept very simple.

A nonformal education campaign which is particularly hopeful is the latest in a series of mass media campaigns devised by the Adult Education Institute in Tanzania. It is entitled 'Chakula ni Uhai' (Food is Life) and is expected to reach 4 million people by means of radio broadcasts, study groups, posters and simple texts. It follows a smaller campaign last year: 'Mtu ni Afya' (Man is Health) which concentrated on hygiene. The important features of the projects are that the message is extremely simple and the emphasis is on immediate practical application, e.g. the present campaign aims to persuade the participants to eat more than once a day, to grow a larger variety of foodstuffs and organize communal catering at places of work, etc.

Nonformal education is a big advance on formal schooling as a means of reaching the rural majority in developing countries, but neither approaches the significance of 'informal' education, i.e. the background experience of each individual from birth which shapes his/her consciousness. Enrichment of the rural environment could thus be a more powerful education medium than expensive and administratively problematic schemes.

Some socialist LDCs are attempting to combine formal education with community service. Agricultural skills are applied and taught in the school grounds and the produce of the children's work is then used to meet school expenses. In China the concept of linking education with grassroots physical work continues to university level and all students are required to spend a proportion of their time in manual labor in the country. The emphasis of education in China is on training large numbers of people to a relatively low level, rather than a handful to be experts. Hence rural health facilities are run by the famous 'bare-foot doctors' who are paramedicals trained to deal with the common health problems of developing countries. Similarly, practical scientific research involves large numbers of ordinary people with the minimum of training. The successful earthquake prediction in February 1975 was largely a result of basic observations by the general population in the vulnerable area.

Population

Is explosive population growth a significant factor in world hunger? The Club of Rome in their report *Limits to Growth* certainly thought so and logically an exponentially growing population must eventually outstrip food supplies as this extract from Allaby's book (1972) clearly shows:

Let us imagine, then, a world without farmers as such, a world which feeds us by producing the maximum amount of green matter possible. We have a large part of the earth's land surface at our disposal and perhaps we can add to this by the cultivation of algae, such as *Chlorella*, which is reputed to be far more efficient than agricultural plants at photosynthesis.

There is an ecological rule of thumb that says that the green plants in a natural ecosystem trap something like 0.1 per cent of the available solar radiation. Herbivores are able to consume some 10 per cent of this – the energy represented by the edible portions of plants – and carnivores have available to them 10 per cent of the energy that was available to the herbivores. From this it has been calculated that mankind has available to it about 1 per cent of the total solar radiation trapped by plants. Edward S. Deevey Jr. has challenged the base figure – the efficiency of land-plant production – and suggests that it should be raised by a factor of three or four. Even then, his estimates may be low; Prof. Newbould's figures are higher than this for Austrian pine forest and for several agricultural plants! His estimate is in the region of 0.6 per cent. If he is right, and if we assume that the whole of this green matter can be processed into foods suitable for humans, then the present population of the earth could increase by up to sixty times – to something like 216 000 million . . . . .
. . . Then, at this density, we would have reached the ultimate limit of human expansion. If it continued unchecked past this point, the whole edifice would collapse. If population continues to increase at its present rate, we will reach this population level in about 200 years!

What then? What do we do when we have reached this final limit? Do we try, somehow, to keep on growing? Do we seeks ways to increase food production still further? How? Do we allow natural events to take their course and suffer a population collapse?

Or do we then, at the last moment of human history, seek ways of stopping growth? If this is a situation we are bound to face, should we wait to face it then, or should we not face it now? In point of fact, do we face it now anyway? (*Reproduced by permission.*)

However, the present food crisis is a result of distribution, not of absolute shortage, and many authorities are convinced that the potential for increasing production is enormous. Furthermore, population pressure is a local, not a global phenomenon. Many African countries, despite a high population growth rate, are sparsely populated, whereas the countries of the Indian subcontinent are highly populous and major cities in any LDC are usually grossly over-populated.

Poor people need large families as children, or more usually sons, are their only means of ensuring some economic security in old age. Birth control campaigns have been notoriously unsuccessful amongst the poor for this reason, and also because of the low status and inaccessibility of women. Most women do not have access to information about contraception, child-bearing is about the only creative activity permitted them and they have a duty to produce sons. An unusual type of 'technological fix' which has been proposed to reduce population growth would cash in on the low status of women. It is a (hypothetical) pill which would ensure conception of male children only. Such a pill, if made freely available, would be most popular among the groups with the highest birth rates and would, of course, redically reduce population growth. However, the social side effects of skewing the sex ratio in this way can only be guessed at and might be disastrous.

Other technological fixes have been suggested, but an increasing number of authorities believe that the population problem is a consequence of poverty and will solve itself when poverty is eliminated. This seems to have been the case in the industrialized world, but can we afford to wait? At the individual level, high fertility is a major cause of malnutrition. Short intervals between pregnancies damage health and nutritional status of both mothers and children and it is these people who make up the bulk of those 462 millions the FAO believe are in imminent danger of starvation.

N.B. The author had hoped to include a reprint of an article by Frances Moore Lappe and Joe Collins from *New Internationalist* (August, 1976) and extract's from Sinha's book *Food and Poverty* (Ch. 5 'Land Reform and the Poor', pp. 48—65). This was not possible for reasons of space, but the interested reader is advized to consult these before considering the discussion questions below.

Points for discussion and general essays

What are your views on the 'Hard' versus 'Soft' technology controversy? Is a compromise possible? Is there such a thing as a 'technological fix' for the problems of rural development? (Papanek, 1974; Schumacher, 1973, 1975)

Is appropriate education the key to rural development? What type of education system would you envisage as suitable, given the problems of shortage of money, poor communications and rural inertia? (Illich, 1971)

Is there a role for Western research in AT for LDCs? Can the well-meaning, skilled Westerner assist development in the field? What are the ethical problems of cultural interference? Is the traditional Christian charitable ideal a help or a hindrance in such work?

What do we mean by the term 'technological infrastructure'? Can you propose alternative methods of providing these services which are cheap and appropriate to the needs of rural industries in LDCs? (Papanek, 1974; Schumacher, 1973, 1975)

The Chinese approach to development is held by many authorities to be the ideal and, as far as we know, malnutrition has been eliminated, and population growth and urbanization controlled in China. What are the reasons for the Chinese success? What are the drawbacks to this system? Is it applicable to other cultures? (Power and Holenstein, 1976; Sinha, 1976)

It is often said that poverty causes the population explosion and that people will automatically limit their own fertility if their economic situation improves. What are the factors which have reduced the birth rate in the industrialized world?

Discuss the impact of the traditional role of women on food production, nutrition, health and population growth in the Third World. What changes in women's situation might assist rural development? Do present development strategies benefit women in LDCs? (Boserup, 1970; Reid, 1976)

Discuss the power of vested interests in the Third World. Numerous examples have been mentioned in this book and you can probably think of others. Can these interests be overcome? Need they be overcome to solve the problem of hunger?

It should be obvious by now that personal ideology plays a large part in consideration of these issues. Are you aware of your own ideological stand in these discussions? Have your views been altered at all by this book? Do you think this book is a fair presentation of the subject? What omissions can you detect? Can you identify the ideology of the author? Could such a presentation be completely objective?

Finally, is there anything that we can do, as voters, consumers, activists, experts or whatever, to improve the nutrition of the world's underprivileged majority?

Reading

Allaby, M. (1972). *Who Will Eat?* Tom Stacey: Prospect for Man Series
Mainly concerned with agricultural and ecological aspects of food, this summarizes the 'environmentalist's' approach to the problem. It may be difficult to get hold of as the publishers recently went out of business and I do not know if it has yet been published elsewhere.

Allaby, M. (1974). 'Fertilizers: the holes in the bag'. *New Scientist* 64 No. 922 (7 November), pp. 402–407

BBC *Horizon* film (1976). *Children of Peru.* BBC Film Library, Reynard Mills, Windmill Road, Brentford, Middx. TW8 9NF (55 minutes)

Berg, A. and Muscat, R. (1972). 'Nutrition and development: the view of the planner. *Am. J. clin. Nutr.*, **25**, pp. 186–209

Blix, G., Hofvander, Y. and Vahlquist, B. (1971). *Famine: a symposium dealing with nutrition and relief operations in times of disaster.* The Swedish Nutrition Foundation Symposium No. IV (26 August) Stockholm

Borgstrom, G. (1973). *World Food Resources.* International Textbook Co. Ltd.
This readable book is a mine of useful information on food production, consumption and trade all over the world. It also covers nutrition, food technology and the logistics and energy requirements of food distribution.

Boserup, E. (1970). *Woman's Role in Economic Development.* London, George Allen & Unwin Ltd.

Boulding, K.E. (1973). Extracts from *A ballad of ecological awareness.* In *The Careless Technology.* Edited by T. Farvar and J.P. Milton. Tom Stacey: Prospect for Man Series, p. 3 and p. 371

Brothwell, D. and Brothwell, P. (1969). *Food in Antiquity: a survey of the diet of early peoples.* London, Thames and Hudson

Donaldson, P. (1973). *Worlds Apart: the economic gulf between nations.* Harmondsworth, Penguin Books
Although not directly concerned with the food problem, this book provides an invaluable insight into the fundamental economic problems facing developing countries. The course of industrialization in Britain and the economic repercussions of imperialism are outlined and it helps to explain the problems facing 'late developers' today and the factors which tend to exacerbate the maldistribution of wealth.

Easlea, B. (1973). *Liberation and the Aims of Science.* Sussex University Press, Chatto and Windus

Ecologist, The (1972). *A Blueprint for Survival.* Harmondsworth, Penguin Books

Follis, R.H. (1963). 'The ecology of hunger'. *Milit. Med.,* **128,** pp. 384–391

Illich, I. (1971). *Deschooling Society.* Calder and Boyar

Luce, H.R. (1966). 'The challenge of the future: an overview'. In *Food and Civilization: A Symposium.* Edited by S.N. Farber, N.L. Wilson and R.H.L. Wilson. Springfield, Charles C. Thomas, pp. 4–16

Manning, D.H. (1976). *Disaster Technology: An Annotated Bibliography.* Oxford, Pergamon Press, pp. 93–137 and 206–211

Manning, D.H. (1975). *Thought for Food.* Paper presented to the British Association for the Advancement of Science annual meeting (1 September)

Manning, D.H. (1976). *Doom for Whom: Decisions in Design.* Paper presented to the Institution of Engineering Designers at a conference on Design for Survival, Chelmsford (July)

Mead, M. (1976). 'Agriculture: Men's work, women's work?' *STPP News* (January), West Lafayette, Indiana, Purdue University

Meadows, D.H., Meadows, D.L., Randers, J. and Behrens, W.W. (1972). *The Limits to Growth.* London, Earth Island Books Ltd

Mellanby, K. (1975). *Can Britain Feed Itself?* London, Merlin Press

Mollison, P.L. (1946). 'Observations on cases of starvation at Belsen'. *Br. med. J.,* **I,** pp. 4–8

Moore Lappe, F. and Collins, J. (1976). 'Food first'. *New Internationalist,* **42** (August), pp. 5–9

Muller, M. (1974). 'Aid, corruption and waste'. *New Scientist,* **64** No. 922 (7 November), pp. 398–400

New Internationalist (1975). **24** (February), p. 1

New Internationalist (1975). **25** (March), p. 1

New Internationalist (1976). **37** (March), p. 24 and 25

New Internationalist (1976). **38** (April), p. 20

Papanek, V. (1974). *Design for the Real World.* Paladin Books
Excellent book for those interested in appropriate technology. New directions in design to meet the needs of developing countries and neglected groups in the rich world are proposed, but the author also exposes the powerful vested interests which tend to block these innovations.

Payne, P. (1974). 'Protein deficiency or starvation?' *New Scientist,* **64** No. 922 (7 November), pp. 393–398

Pirie, N.W. (1976). *Food Resources: Conventional and Novel.* Harmondsworth, Penguin Books
Useful, cheap and readable book relevant to all sections of this book.

Power, J. and Holenstein, A-M. (1976). *World of Hunger: A Strategy for Survival.* Maurice Temple Smith Ltd.

The book is mainly concerned with the economic and agricultural aspects of world food. The section on urbanization and migrant labor is excellent and a useful chapter entitled 'Seven countries' gives a brief outline of the different approaches to development of Japan, Tanzania, Brazil, Eire, Bangladesh, The Philippines and China.

Pyke, M. (1968). *Food and Society*. London, John Murray

Pyke, M. (1970). *Man and Food*. World University Library
This is a useful and entertaining general introduction to a study of food and nutrition. The social and cultural aspects of diet are discussed. The section on nutritional science provides a concise, illustrated summary of the discovery of the vitamins, deficiency diseases and nutritional requirements. A section on food technology, covering preservation techniques, mechanization in farming and synthetic food sources is included. The final section on food and health is rather speculative, but raises interesting questions concerning the definition of good nutrition and the factors influencing population size.

Reid, E. (1976). 'The long walk'. *New Internationalist*, 43 (September), pp. 18–19

Ritson, C. (1975). 'Should Britain feed itself?' *New Society* (27 November), pp. 479–481

Sahlvis, M. (1974). 'The original affluent society'. *The Ecologist*, 4 No. 5 (June), pp. 181–189

Schumacher, E.F. (1975). *Small is Beautiful*. Bland and Briggs Ltd. (1973); Sphere Books
This was the book which started the movement for alternative technology in rural development. It also proposes a new ideology in economic planning, applicable to the industrialized world also and summarized by the book's subtitle: A study of economics as if people mattered'.
The literature of the Intermediate Technology Development Group, founded by Schumacher, may also be useful. ITDG, Parnell House, Wilton Road, London SW1.

Shell Films (1970). *Food or Famine*. Shell Film Library, 25 The Burroughs, Hendon, London NW4 (30 minutes). Available for nominal fee.

Sinha, R. (1976). *Food and Poverty*. Croom Helm Ltd.
For a short, readable book, this is remarkably comprehensive. It is an economist's view and its coverage of world trade, development aid, land reform and employment is particularly useful. A good critique of nutritional assessment methods is included in an appendix. Highly recommended, this book is well worth reading in its entirety.

Tannahill, R. (1975). *Food in History*. Paladin Books

Wagstaff, H. (1976). *World Food: A Political Task*. Fabian Research

Series 26, Fabian Society, 11 Dartmouth Street, London SW1
Woodham Smith, C. (1964). *The Great Hunger: Ireland 1845–9.*
London, Readers Union, Hamish Hamilton